Simulation and Path Planning Techniques for Static Obstacle Avoidance in Autonomous Robots

By

Martin Vlog

Contents

Chapter 1

Introduction

1.1 Industrial Revolutions

The First Industrial Revolution happened in Europe and America during the 18th to 19th century. During this period, primarily rural, agrarian societies became urban and industrial. Along with the steam engine, the textile and iron industries played vital roles in the First Industrial Revolution. Charles Beard [1] presented in his book the socio-economic conditions before and after the First Industrial Revolution.

The Second Industrial Revolution took place around First World War. It was a time of evolution for new factories and expanding of the existing ones. Using electricity, steel and oil industries created mass production. Light bulbs, phonographs, telephone, and the IC engine are significant technological advances during this period. Ruth Scwarz Cowan [2] explains the change in technology that can be used to reduce household works because of the Industrial Revolution 2.0. David A Collier [3] presents the implications of the simultaneous automation of goods and services on the workers and actions taken to smooth the transition in the United States. Britannica Encyclopaedia [4] shows how Industrial Revolution 2.0 crossed Britain and Europe and changed the world's lifestyle.

The Third Industrial Revolution mentions the furtherance of technology from analogue electronic devices and mechanical devices to the current day digital world. This is called Digitalization, which gained prominence around the eighties and is continuing. Preferences during the third Industrial Revolution are the personal desktop computer, the World Wide Web - internet, and information and communications technology. Lynn A Karoly et al. [5 to 7] presented in detail the advent of the information age and rapid space of technology advances (Moore's law), real private fixed investment in Information Technology. They presented the change in the world's relationship to community, time, craftsmanship, and human's own role in society.

The Fourth Industrial Revolution raises on the digitalisation presenting state-of-art ways in which embedded technology is seen in every place, including the body of human beings. This fourth industrial revolution is distinct by a number of emerging technology innovations in almost all the fields, some to mention Nanotechnology, the Internet of Things, Driverless cars, Robotics, Artificial Intelligence, Biotechnology, 3D Printing, Quantum Computing, etc. The Fourth Industrial revolution is designated by a mix of hybrid technologies that is erasing the lines between the digital, biological and physical spheres.

Robotics is having a significant role in Industrial Revolution 4.0. Even a minimal improvement in the field of Robotics will have a significant impact on humanity. A brief history of Robotics is enumerated hereunder.

1.2 Robotics

Multidisciplinary nature is the most set a part feature of Robotics. To design an excellent robotic system, an engineer must possess knowledge about control engineering, computer engineering, mechanical engineering, industrial engineering, electrical engineering, along with business and economics.

Engineers, through best design procedures and scrupulous observation of details, have flourished in pertaining the science of robotics to a wide range of manufacturing and industrial problems. From a practical standpoint, robots are different from conventional electromechanical motion equipment by their handling abilities, in that robots can operate, position, and move tools and other items with far greater competence than other manufacturing machines.

The automobile sector in the United States was the first to successfully implement process robots on a commercial scale. Mass production of automobiles is no longer possible while respecting the quality and cost levels currently accepted without the use of robots. In early 1995, there were more than 25,000 robots in the American auto industry. Spot welding is the most common application for these robots. For all applications and industries, the global requirement for robots is expected to surpass one million units by 1999.

1.2.1 Description of Robotics

In 1975, robotic microprocessor controllers made it practical and reliable to program and execute coordinated movements of complex robots with multiple degrees of freedom (DOF). The robot industry has proliferated, and humans have been replaced in a number of manufacturing processes involving the handling of tools and/or work pieces.

Roboticists are concerned with the development of artificial mechanical devices capable of moving by themselves, the movement of which must be modelled, planned, detected, controlled and activated, whose movement behaviour can be influenced by 'programming'. When robots are able to move safely in an unstructured environment while executing their given tasks autonomously, they are referred to as "intelligent."

"A robot is a reprogrammable, autonomously controlled, multifunctional manipulator with equal to or more than three axes," according to the International Organization for Standardization.

"A robot is a reprogrammable-multifunctional manipulator that moves tools, components, material, and other objects through various programmed movements for the execution of a range of tasks", according to the Robot Institute of America.

Robotics is mostly about system integration, or the completion of a task with the aid of an actuated mechanical device and the "smart" integration of components, many of which are shared with other areas. Because basic technologies from diverse domains are essential components in current robotic systems, the boundaries of robotics are challenging to define.

1.2.2 Mythological Influence on Robotics

Mythology is full of fabricated beings in every culture. According to Greek tradition, Cadmus defeated the dragon that had slain many of his friends after founding Thebes, and Cadmus sowed the dragon's teeth into the soil, from which a formidable army of armed men grew.

The golem, a clay or stone figure thought to hold a scroll with religious or magical powers that animate it, is introduced in Jewish mythology; the golem performs repetitive and straightforward duties, but it is difficult to stop.

1.2.3 Motion Pictures Influence on Robotics

The advent of cinematic images such as "Metropolis" "The Day the Earth Stood Still" presented some of these mythical creatures, combined with an ostensibly limitless supply of new artificial creatures. Many robots have appeared in films and television shows, playing both evil and heroic characters. While this is only a tiny sampling, it demonstrates humans' fascination with mechanical animals.

1.2.4 Inventions and their Influence on Robotics

In 1801, a Frenchman named Joseph Jacquard created a loom that used a sequence of punched cards to control the repetition of patterns used to weave linen and carpets. Charles Babbage used Jacquard's card method to construct an automated calculator in early nineteenth-century Britain, the concepts of which ultimately led to the creation of computers and computer programming.

Seventy years before General Motors debuted its first industrial robot, Seward Babbitt constructed a motorised crane with a mechanical gripper to retrieve ingots from a furnace. Nikola Tesla, who is most renowned for his discoveries in AC electric power, the radio, induction motors, and other disciplines, built the first remote-controlled vehicle, a radio-controlled watercraft, in the 1890s. On November 8, 1898, Tesla received Patent #613.809 for his discoveries.

1.2.5 "Robot" Word – First Use

Until the 1920s, industrialists, let alone science fiction authors, had never heard of the phrase "robot." Rossum's Universal Robots was written by Karel C apek (1890–1938) in 1920. (R U R). C Apek went to his elder brother, Josef, for a name for these entities while he composed his play. Josef responded with a new term he coined: Robot. A peasant or serf is referred to as a Robotnik in Czech, whereas robota refers to hardship or slavery.

1.2.6 First Use of the word "Robotics"

Another science fiction author with a cult following a significant effect on robotics history was Isaac Asimov (1920–1992). He wrote a series of short stories with a robot theme. Asimov presented what would become known as the "Three Laws of Robotics" in his short tales.

1.3 Types of Robots

1.3.1 Industrial Robots

As per International Standards Organization, An industrial robot is a multifunctional manipulator with three or more axes that can be operated automatically and reprogrammed. They are currently employed in a variety of industrial applications. Robots are considerably better at occupations that require accuracy, repetition, dependability, endurance, and speed. As a result, many industrial occupations previously performed by people are increasingly being performed by robots. Dispensing activities, welding, assembling, painting, palletising and packing items, laboratory applications, and printed circuit boards are among the industrial occupations that robots do.

1.3.2 Robots Used In Agriculture

Although the idea of robots planting seeds, ploughing fields, and harvesting crops may seem like something out of a science fiction novel, there are several agricultural robots in the experimental stages of development, such as robots that can pick apples, prune grapevines, transplant seedlings, and so on.

1.3.3 Tele-Robots

Tele-robots are employed in locations where people are hazardous, inaccessible, or too far away to be managed by a human operator. It is possible that it will come in handy if you are dealing with hazardous materials or doing activities that might be dangerous to humans.

1.3.4 Robots in Service Sector

Outside of an industrial facility, robots are categorised as one of two types: robots that are used for professional tasks and robots that are utilised for personal purposes. Many service industries, including tourist hubs, hospitals, retail malls, and hotels, use robots to assist their clients.

1.3.5 Nano Robots

Robots, the size of a few nanometres, is Nanobots, which can be used in different applications. Nanobots are designed to execute particular biological functions in the context of medicine, and when injected into the blood, they work on cancer cells or any other damaged cells. Nanobots combined with biological research will usher in a new era in medical research.

1.3.6 Robots in Medical Sector

Medical robots that can do surgeries are becoming increasingly popular, and surgical robots are being developed and tested in two areas. Tele-robotics, for example, allows a doctor to do surgery from afar. Minimally invasive surgery, on the other hand, entails doing surgery without making large incisions.

1.3.7 Virtual Robots

In reality, virtual robots do not exist. Virtual robots are nothing more than software building components in a computer. A virtual robot might resemble a real robot or just do a routine activity.

1.4 Mobile Robots

For a variety of reasons, autonomous mobile robot research is fascinating. Using on-bot sensors, the first mobile robot can only perceive some physical aspects of the environment. Current mobile robots are intelligent enough to detect patterns and regularities, identify features, localise, build maps to navigate, and even learn from their experiences. These robots need a simultaneous application in many research fields.

Computer science and engineering are essential elements of mobile robots, evidently, but when questions of smart working arise, cognitive science, artificial intelligence, philosophy and psychology offer solutions.

Surveillance, inspection, transportation, and house cleaner robots are among commercial uses for mobile robots. In their papers, Weigl M et al. [15 to 17] covered the mechanical, motor, sensory, perceptual, and cognitive aspects of mobile robots. In these works, authors discuss both fresh breakthroughs and advancements in robot route planning, as well as state-of-the-art approaches.

Mobile robots have yet to have a significant impact in industrial and household applications due to a lack of dependability, adaptable navigation and behaviour systems and robustness. The main drawback is semi-structured, unmodified environs. One solution is to use markers such as beacons, visual patterns or induction loops. However, this is rigid, costly, and sometimes impossible. Alternative navigation in unmodified settings necessitates the use of advanced sensor signal processing techniques that are yet in beta stages. Another significant reason for building intelligent, autonomous robots is to allow mobile robots to work in regions that are inaccessible to people or to do repetitive, arduous, or dangerous activities. Michael Decker [8] described robot navigation as a set of tasks that comprise perception, collecting and interpreting sensory data, exploration, mapping, localisation, path planning, path execution, and so on.

Finally, mobile robots have an artistic and aesthetic quality to them. Swarms of robots assemble to execute a specific task or to avoid colliding with one another and objects in their environment. In his book, William A Pelz [7] discusses developments in mobile robotics and associated technologies used in the design and development of multi-robot systems. He detailed the development of safe and secure control software and control strategies of a human interactive robot as in the case of a robotic wheelchair. Textbook from Carnegie Mellon Robotics Academy explains how the mathematics, science, technology and communication is applied to robots depending upon various application like the speed, acceleration, distance travelled. This book explains how to collect data, examine the behaviour of a mobile robot

1.4.1 Autonomous Robots

Self-contained or, to put it another way, self-supporting autonomous robots are self-contained. They rely on their own intelligence in certain respects. Autonomous robots follow software that allows them to choose which action to take based on their environment. These robots can even learn new behaviours.

1.4.2 Remote-Control Robots

An autonomous robot is not the ideal solution if a robot must do increasingly complex yet unknown jobs. Human scores against robots in solving complicated tasks with actual brainpower. A human may do complex and typically dangerous jobs without physically being at the task area by remotely instructing a robot. To explode a bomb, for example, sending the robot to the danger zone is preferable.

1.4.3 Mobility

Mobile robots, which are moving on a planar surface, are called two-dimensional mobile robots. These are also called land robots or terrestrial robots. Mobile robots that are moving in space are called three-dimensional mobile robots. These are also called space robots, copter robots, or underwater robots.

1.4.4 Applications of Mobile Robots

Some applications of mobile robots are space explorations; service sectors like hospitals, hotels, and schools; defence and surveillance sectors like police, military; emergency response teams to deal with hazardous situations; transportation; industry; home robots; medical field; entertainment; inspection and maintenance etc.

1.4.4.1 Industrial Applications

Automation in the delivery/logistic and warehousing/fulfilment chains is growing in popularity. The use of mobile robots and autonomous vehicles to automate movement-based tasks, such as autonomous cars and robots, delivery robots, automated goods-to-person robots, mobile picking robots, autonomous and collaborative robots, autonomous trucks and vans, autonomous material handling vehicles such as taggers and forklifts, and last-mile delivery, is a fascinating subset of this. This subject covers a wide range of drones, robots, and self-driving vehicles that assist products in their trip from the initial point to the point of destination.

1.4.4.2 Medical Applications

Autonomous mobile robots travel long distances in hospital hallways transporting patients, medications, patient meals, medical supplies, linens, etc. and can be used to collect the trash. Figures 1.1 and 1.2 show robots used in hospitals.

1.4.4.3 Defence Applications

Defence robots are self-contained robots or remote-controlled devices used in military operations. Defence robots include military transportation robots, search and rescue robots, fire fighting robots, mine clearance robots, surveillance and reconnaissance robots, armed military robots, unmanned aerial vehicle (UAV) robots, and unmanned ground vehicles (UGV) robots.

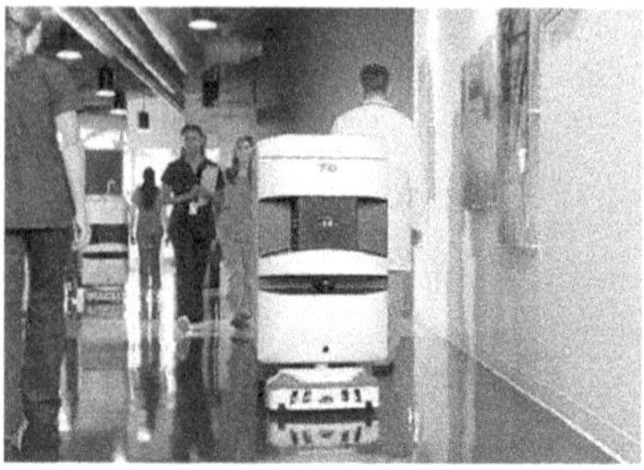

a. Goods Carrying Robot b. Sanitisation Robot

Figure 1.1: Mobile Robots in Medical Field (Courtesy: Aethon Inc, XAG)

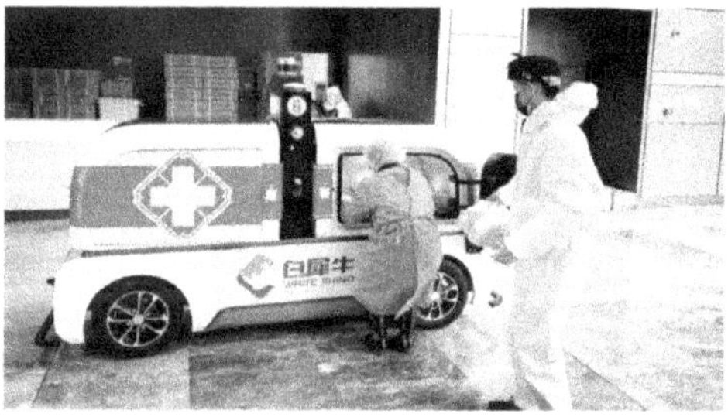

Figure 1.2: Autonomous Ambulance (Courtesy: White Rhino)

1.4.4.3.1 Tasks Handled By Military Robots

Some of the tasks handled by military robots are: a. Reconnaissance and mapping are particularly crucial in large-scale rescue operations resulting from natural catastrophes. b. Aiding rescue missions in urban search and rescue situations c. Rubble removal in calamities and aid in victim extraction. d. Tele-presence and e. Logistics

1.4.4.3.2 Cargo Carriers

These are military robots that perform transportation tasks. It may be anything from ammunition to weapons to supplies. For rugged terrain, they can be legged robots, but in general, most are wheeled robots. Successful warfare has always relied heavily on logistics. Military transportation robots can improve logistical efficiency while also assisting soldiers in their mobility. At the end of the day, causalities must be determined. Robots can take the place of humans in all of these dangerous scenarios.

1.4.4.3.3 Autonomous Platform Demonstrator

The APD (Autonomous Platform Demonstrator) is a military transportation robot created by the TARDEC (Tank Automotive Research, Development and Engineering Centre) of the United States Army. It is a 9.6-ton hybrid-electric UGV with six in-hub electric motors driven by Li-ion batteries charged by an onboard diesel generator. The APD is a skid steer capable of pivoting and turning in situ. A lightweight hull, an improved suspension system, and other innovations are included.

1.4.4.3.4 iRobot Warrior

The iRobot Warrior is a military robot with several functions. It can carry a payload of around 70 kg. This enables it to be utilised for a variety of purposes, including the evacuation of casualties and the transfer of hazardous items. Its primary benefit is its adaptability. It can navigate 45-degree stairwells and slopes, as well as gaps of up to 61 cm and vertical impediments of up to 47 cm. It is designed to be utilised both on rugged terrain and in urban areas.

1.4.4.3.5 MULE

The acronym MULE refers to a multipurpose utility/logistics and equipment vehicle. Lockheed Martin is also working on this one. It is supposed to have a few different versions. Two infantry squads' worth of equipment and supplies may be carried by the transport variant of the mule. It may be adapted to transport practically any type of cargo, even casualties.

1.4.4.3.6 Search and Rescue Robots

In search and rescue efforts, robots are utilised. Despite the fact that robots are not frequently employed in actual search and rescue scenarios now, the future of this sector appears bright. At first glance, things appear to be relatively straightforward; robots capable of penetrating debris mounds and locating individuals behind them are required. Robots might be used in a variety of settings and to perform a variety of jobs.

1.4.4.3.7 Fire-fighting Robots

Many things might go wrong and affect a specific segment of the population. Wildfires, tsunamis, earthquakes, and man-made calamities like Chernobyl or 9/11 are all possibilities.

Urban Search Rescue (US&R, USAR), Wide Area Search and Rescue (WASAR) are the two most prevalent scenarios. Both an earthquake and a bomber run can trigger a USAR scenario.

Natural catastrophes such as floods and wildfires, on the other hand, are frequently the cause of large-scale search and rescue operations.

It is possible that this dangerous profession will one day be delegated to robots. There are currently active initiatives involving robots that can be linked to a fire hydrant and used to fight fires. Fire fighting robots have the potential to save many lives in the future, the lives of individuals who have been impacted by a fire, as well as those who serve as firefighters. Despite the fact that this day has not yet arrived, research activities in this sector are pushing things forward every year.

1.4.4.3.8 Hoya Fire-fighters' Assistance Robot

This robot, created by the Hoya Robot Company and supported by the South Korean government, is intended to be used by firefighters as a personal spy. Despite its thick armour and tough appearance, it only has a diameter of 12.5 cm and weighs 2 kilos.

This robotic gadget can be dropped into a burning building and run for 30 minutes. Firefighters may use this remote-controlled robot to investigate the surroundings and plan their operations accordingly because it can endure temperatures up to 160^0 C (320^0 F).

1.4.4.3.9 DRB Fatec Archibots

Another Korean robotics firm is DRB Fatec. Two firefighting robots have been developed because of research and development activities. These are ArchiBot-M and ArchiBot-S, respectively. Both robots can climb and descend stairs, are waterproof and feature a cooling system that allows them to function in hot environments. The ArchiBot-M is significantly bigger than the ArchiBot-S, weighing 450 kg vs 40 kg. It also goes quicker (20 km/h vs 8 km/h) and has a more extended operational period (2 hours vs 1 hour). While both may be used to explore the site, ArchiBot-M has the ability to battle fires on its own

1.4.4.3.10 Mine Clearance Robots

Another expedition that poses a high risk of human death is land mines. Today, mine-clearing military robots are employed all over the world. A remote operator generally operates these robots from a safe distance.

1.4.4.3.11 Surveillance and Reconnaissance Robots

Knowing what the competitor has up his sleeve is a huge advantage. Various robots carry out surveillance and/or reconnaissance operations. Military robots deployed for surveillance operations behind enemy lines might be armed.

1.4.4.3.12 Unmanned Ground Vehicles

An unmanned ground vehicle (UGV) is a military robot, which helps soldiers perform better. This sort of robot can often operate outside and over a broad range of terrain, taking the role of people. Unmanned aerial vehicles (UAVs) and naval warfare both have UGV equivalents (remotely operated underwater vehicles). Unmanned robots are being developed for tedious, dirty, and hazardous jobs for both civilian and military uses.

1.4.4.4 Other Fields

Many employments in manufacturing, agriculture, and entertainment necessitate tedious, monotonous work requiring a high level of precision. Robots are better adapted to such situations than humans since they are accurate, clever, and do not become tired like humans. Some tasks are hazardous and harmful for humans, such as space and undersea exploration. Robots are also ideal for this situation because they are never weary. Because of these benefits, robots have a wide range of applications in practically all industries. Some areas like agriculture, retail, manufacturing, logistics and delivery, public transportation, commercial freight transport, security, space exploration, entertainment, and mining are some mong these businesses.

1.4.4.5 Aerial Robots

Remote sensing, picture gathering, transportation, disaster response, surveillance, and delivery of products are just a few of the possible uses for robots with the amount of mobility provided by flight.

Aerial robots' military uses have been known since the dawn of powered flight, and they have already been implemented to remarkable success in surveillance, targeting, and even striking operations. An unmanned aerial vehicle (UAV) is an aircraft, which is not piloted and does not have a human crew on board. Their primary application is in military applications. Military unmanned aerial vehicles (UAVs) are carrying out reconnaissance and attack operations.

Disaster response, surveillance, remote sensing, transportation, picture capture, and delivery of commodities are just a few of the civilian uses. One best example, which is in discussion everywhere, is a delivery drone, often an unmanned autonomous aerial vehicle (UAV), used to transport packages, food or other goods.

1.4.4.6 Underwater Robots

Underwater Robots are vehicles, which move under the water in a three-dimensional path. Underwater Robots are one of the most advanced technologies available today for oceanographic research.

1.4.4.6.1 Autonomous/Unmanned Underwater Vehicle

Any vehicle that can operate underwater without a human occupant is referred to as an unmanned underwater vehicle (UUV). Autonomous Underwater Vehicles (AUV) provide tasks such as oceanography, surveillance, and reconnaissance (ISR), inspection and identification, mine countermeasures, intelligence and payload delivery for the Navy. Some of the biggest AUVs can carry out assault missions, including anti-submarine warfare and time-critical attacks.

When a ship's hull is damaged at sea, it is critical to get repairs done as soon as possible. Repair teams want efficient solutions that are tailored to current difficulties in these situations, when even minutes may make a significant impact. AUVs make this task simple. Some other application fields of AUVs are underwater photography, underwater excavation operations etc.

1.4.4.7 Special Cases

Some exceptional cases in three-dimensional robots are like Big Dog legged robots. Boston Dynamics developed the Big Dog. Even when kicked from the side, it can maintain its equilibrium. It can travel where other wheeled and treaded robots cannot because of its walking skills. Hydraulics are utilised to move its legs, and a diesel engine powers the hydraulic pump.

1.4.4.8 Pros, Cons and Limitations

Pros

1. The most significant advantage of employing robots in the workplace is their return on investment. They are substantially less expensive than humans are, and their cost is decreasing.
2. Even though they cannot compete with human abilities, robotic capabilities are rapidly expanding.
3. Robots are significantly more productive than humans are since they are more active and do not tire as easily.
4. They are more precise than humans are.
5. Advanced robots outperform humans in terms of strength and speed.
6. They come in any size and shape, depending upon the requirement.
7. Robots can work in any environmental situation, including underwater, in space, in high heat, cold, or wind, and so on. They can be utilised everywhere when human safety is a major concern.
8. Robots cannot say no to anything, and they may be employed for any unpleasant or risky task that people would refuse to do.
9. Robots are very successful in warfare and are saving more human lives.

10. In the Chemical industry, which is a major health concern for humans, robots are the best alternative.
11. Robots are more precise than human beings are.

Cons

1. Robots are a major concern for unemployment.
2. Robots working in industries still require manual labour to coordinate.
3. Robots have no conscience or emotions. They make the workplace emotionless because of a lack of empathy.

Limitations

1. Robots can unquestionably handle their prescribed job, but they typically cannot handle unpredicted situations.
2. They have Artificial Intelligence, but they are unquestionably not as smart as human beings are.
3. They can never perform their tasks outside the pre-defined programming.

According to the International Federation of Robotics, global sales of industrial robots will reach 500,000 units by 2019, with South Korea and the automotive sector leading the way in terms of country and sector, respectively. Inkwoodresearch.com predicted the robotics market across several sectors and robot kinds. Articulated robots will account for a significant portion of the worldwide industrial robotics market. According to a PricewaterhouseCoopers report from 2017, companies are willing to invest 31% in robotics over the next five years. According to a JP Morgan survey, robotics is one of the top five technologies influencing human lifestyle by 2025. On the other hand, automation and robotics have put approximately 40% of jobs in the United States in jeopardy.

1.5 Mobile Robot Navigation

Mobile robots frequently work in unfamiliar, hostile, desolate, uninhabited, dangerous, and unpleasant locations in most applications. These robots must be able to continually monitor their environs and respond appropriately to variety and unpredictability. Every autonomous mobile robot must execute the essential job of securely moving from one location to another within its surroundings. Mobile robot navigation involves four basic sub-problems: Mapping, Localisation, Path Planning, and Motion Control. The convolution of addressing mobile navigation at a higher level leads to a common practice of decomposing the problem into sensory-based/local and map-based/global navigation. Sensory-based local navigation focuses primarily on path planning and motion control, whereas global navigation focuses on mapping, localisation, and path planning.

The process of concurrently monitoring the location of a mobile robot relative to its surroundings, localisation and mapping are terms used to describe the procedure to build a map of the surroundings. Path planning and motion control are the other two sub-problems that assist the mobile robot in completing navigation tasks. Path planning refers to a mobile robot's capacity to plan its motion in its working environment, whereas motion control implies a mobile robot's capability to follow or track a planned motion.

1.5.1 Motion Planning

Motion planning is also used in non-robotics fields such as visual animation and video game software, minimally invasive surgery planning, etc. This fundamental motion planning problem has several extensions, such as optimised computing trajectories, kinematic and dynamic constraints limiting robot motions, or coordinating multiple robots.

Schwartz T J et al. [14] briefs the fundamentals of motion planning by pointing out the problems generally associated with autonomous robots and different methods of essential motion planning in automated robots. Weigl M et al. [15 and 16], in their paper, explained the need for motion planning and the main aspects of motion planning by illustrating examples in different situations. While ‘path planning' refers to the geometry issue of computing a collision-free way for a robot amid static obstacles, ‘motion planning' refers to difficulties including time, dynamic constraints, object coordination, sensory interaction, and so on.

1.5.2 Path Planning

Mobile robot path planning is one problem that has intrigued and has received much attention throughout robotics history. A mobile robot must be capable of generating anti-collision paths to move from one site to another. These pathways must be optimised under specific parameters that are most essential to the terrain. Navigation or Trajectory Planning [12] deals with the need for trajectory planning and the distinct constraints that should be considered for the different planning algorithms. Maximilian Papa et al. [62] brief the need for mobile robots in automated industrial environments by presenting a summary of the research advances in path planning for a mobile robot in both offline and online settings.

The path planning for the movement of a robot along a planar arena is termed two-dimensional path planning. As mentioned in [17 and 19], the height, weight, shape, and other physical parameters of the robot do not have any influence on two-dimensional path planning. Robots that are skilful at moving along a given plane are called planar robots. Noboria H et. al. [18 and 20] explains how the movement of the robot is confined to two dimensions.

1.5.3 Path Planning Techniques

Path planning, also known as trajectory planning, is divided into two categories: local trajectory planning and global trajectory planning. The degree of knowledge the robot has (either partially known or unknown) about its navigational environment is limited by the local trajectory planning technique. However, in the case of global trajectory planning, the robot has a comprehensive understanding of the navigation environment and can thus follow the planned path to the destination.

However, global trajectory planning methodologies have limited applications as they lack robustness due to uncertainty in terrain data. In contrast, the local trajectory planning techniques have greater flexibilities when there is an incompleteness in data about the environments and offer an optimised route to reach the local target [22]. It can be further divided into the heuristic approach (Artificial Intelligence method) and conventional approach. Mobile robot trajectory planning finds its application in surgical and restorative uses, personal service, security, storage, and circulatory applications, maritime and extra-terrestrial investigations, robot-guided vehicles for transporting goods in a factory, and self-guided explosive transfer and outer planetary investigation robots. Table 1.1 shows different types of path planning techniques along with their year of introduction.

Table 1.1: Different Path Planning Techniques

<table>
<tr><th>S No</th><th colspan="2">Type of the Path Planning Technique</th><th>Name of the Technique</th><th>Introduction Year</th></tr>
<tr><td>1</td><td colspan="2" rowspan="8">Classical Methods</td><td>Potential Field</td><td>1979</td></tr>
<tr><td>2</td><td>Roadmap Cell Decomposition</td><td>1987</td></tr>
<tr><td>3</td><td>Grid Based</td><td>1988</td></tr>
<tr><td>4</td><td>Probabilistic Roadmap (PRM)</td><td>1996</td></tr>
<tr><td>5</td><td>Rapidly Exploring Random Tree</td><td>1998</td></tr>
<tr><td>6</td><td>Virtual Impedance Method</td><td>2000</td></tr>
<tr><td>7</td><td>Convex Hull and Local Search Method</td><td>2001</td></tr>
<tr><td>8</td><td>Divide and Conquer Method</td><td>2001</td></tr>
<tr><td>9</td><td rowspan="9">Reactive/Heuristic Methods</td><td rowspan="3">Artificial Intelligent Methods</td><td>Neural Network Techniques</td><td>1943</td></tr>
<tr><td>10</td><td>Fuzzy Logic Techniques</td><td>1965</td></tr>
<tr><td>11</td><td>Genetic Algorithm Techniques</td><td>1989</td></tr>
<tr><td>12</td><td rowspan="6">Bio-inspired Methods</td><td>Ant Colony Optimization Technique</td><td>1992</td></tr>
<tr><td>13</td><td>Particle Swarm Optimization Technique</td><td>1995</td></tr>
<tr><td>14</td><td>Bacterial Foraging Optimization</td><td>2002</td></tr>
<tr><td>15</td><td>Bee Colony Optimization Technique</td><td>2005</td></tr>
<tr><td>16</td><td>Firefly Algorithm Optimization Technique</td><td>2008</td></tr>
<tr><td>17</td><td>Grey Wolf Optimization</td><td>2014</td></tr>
</table>

There are different trajectory planning techniques of which robot trajectory planning is vital for the design of navigational control. The robot must achieve the target configuration while simultaneously minimising the time and distance traversed. The other criteria, less power consumption and less computational complexity are only feasible if the robot takes the shortest path from its initial configuration to its goal.

Initially, classical methods were used to solve robot-navigating challenges because artificial intelligence techniques had not yet been established. When employing classical methods to complete a task, it is noticed that either a result is obtained or it is confirmed that a result does not exist. The main disadvantage of this strategy is its high processing cost and failure to respond to environmental unpredictability.

Of late, reactive approaches such as genetic algorithm, fuzzy logic, neural network, firefly algorithm, particle swarm optimization, ant colony optimization, bacterial foraging optimization, artificial bee colony, cuckoo search, shuffled frog leaping algorithm, and other miscellaneous algorithms such as invasive weed optimization, harmony search algorithm, bat algorithm, differential evolution algorithm have been developed. They have an extraordinary ability to deal with the ambiguity that exists in the environment.

Table 1.2: Robot Path Planning Simulators

S No	Simulator	Company	Introduction Year
1	Webots®	Cyberbotics®	1998
2	Robotics Developer Studio	Microsoft®	2006
3	ROS®	ROS®	2007
4	V-REP®	Coppelia Robotics®	2013
5	MoveIT®	ROS®	2014
6	Robosim®	UCDavis®	2016
7	Robotics Toolbox	Matlab®	2019

1.6 Obstacles

Nowadays, more and more autonomous mobile robots are being developed and deployed in factory automation and in service sectors. A mobile robot is an autonomous vehicle provided with an intelligent computer to perform given tasks in its environment. For performing their assigned tasks, the robots have to move within the specified environment without colliding with other objects. These objects, which are treated as obstacles in the path of the robot, maybe of static or dynamic in nature. Static obstacles are process equipment, storage bins, in-process inventories etc., on a shop floor. Dynamic obstacles are the other mobile robots, which are performing the same kind of tasks or different tasks. Impediments for three-dimensional robots, particularly underwater, are stones, small underwater hills, and other moving robots. The primary path planning problem is to create a path for a robot that is free of collisions in the presence of both static and dynamic barriers.

1.7 Path Planning Simulators

Path planning simulator is application software that allows users to create simulated routes for mobile robots. Companies such as Matlab®, Microsoft®, and Coppelia Robotics®, among others, created simulators to evaluate path planning for two-dimensional and three-dimensional pathways of mobile robots. Simulators for robot path planning are included in Table 1.2.

1.8 Problem Definition

Finding the shortest and safest path for an autonomous robot is the major problem faced by engineers. Classical (Mathematical) path planning techniques can be explored to find the shortest path in a global environment. Even though reactive techniques have gained popularity in the last two decades in implementing the path planning techniques in real-time robots, they make the robots bulky because of more electronic components. Many researchers tried to develop new reactive techniques, especially bio-inspired techniques. A limited investigation carried on mathematical protocols for planar and spatial techniques for a robot's collision avoidance path and meagre research on comparing classical and reactive techniques, their pros and cons. Hence, there is a need to develop new mathematical protocols for the robot traversing in a two-dimensional or three-dimensional arena and compare the results with reactive technique experimentation and simulation.

1.9 The Objective of the Work

This study reports new mathematical protocols to find the shortest collision avoidance path for the robot. Throughout the literature, no comparative study was found between classical path planning techniques with reactive experimental results. This study showcases reactive experimental and simulation results for the robot's shortest path and compares them with the proposed mathematical protocol results.

The present research mainly focused on developing new novel mathematical protocols for obstacle avoidance path planning for a single robot moving on a planar environment with static elliptical obstacles, elliptical-polygonal obstacles; for two identical robots moving in a planar environment; for a single robot moving in a three-dimensional underwater environment with a cylindrical obstacle. The results obtained from the mathematical protocols were cross-checked with experimental and simulation results. Reactive approach-based experimentations were conducted. Application software is used to simulate the paths. Finally, a comparative study is carried out between the results obtained in all three formats, i.e., mathematical approach, experimental approach, and simulation.

1.10 Organization of the Thesis

Including the "Introduction" chapter, this dissertation is divided into nine chapters.

Chapter-1 deals with the introduction to industrial revolutions, robots, history of the robots. Further, this chapter introduces the concept of mobile robots, types of mobile robots, their application fields. The second part of this chapter introduces types of path planning techniques, i.e., classical and reactive, limitations of both the techniques and their application fields. Followed by an introduction to bio-inspired path planning techniques are discussed in this chapter. The difficulties of AUVs (Autonomous Underwater Vehicles) are also discussed in this chapter. The simulators available for path planning are introduced in this chapter. The last part of this chapter presents the problem definition, objective of the present research work, and organisation of the thesis.

Chapter-2 describes the general review of literature on robots, path planning of the robots. This chapter emphasises the review of the literature concerned with the classical and reactive types of path planning techniques. Literature relevant to classical path planning techniques, reactive path planning techniques, bio-inspired path planning techniques, AUV's are reviewed in this chapter.

The objective and methodology adopted for the present investigation are derived from the thorough literature review. This chapter also describes the problem identification and objective of the present investigation.

Chapter-3 stipulates the methodology adopted to execute the present investigation. Novel mathematical protocols for both two-dimensional and three-dimensional (2.5D) techniques are proposed in this chapter. Experimentation methodology to find out 1) a two-dimensional planar path for the robot with static obstacles like ellipses, polygons, and or combination, 2) a collision-free two-dimensional planar path for two identical robots moving in the same environment, and 3) to find out a path for a robot moving in a three-dimensional underwater environment are proposed in this chapter. A simulator to calculate the paths for all two-dimensional and three-dimensional cases is proposed in this chapter.

Chapters-4 presents the results obtained for the two-dimensional path calculation of a robot against static elliptical obstacles. The results obtained from the respective proposed mathematical protocol, simulator, and experiment are compared. Four test cases (1 to 4) are presented in this chapter.

Chapters-5 presents the results obtained for the two-dimensional path calculation of a robot against static mixed obstacles. The results obtained from the respective proposed mathematical protocol, simulator, and experiment are compared. Seven test cases (5 to 11) are presented in this chapter.

Chapters-6 presents the results obtained for the two-dimensional path calculation of a robot against a dynamic obstacle. The results obtained are from the respective proposed mathematical protocol, simulator, and experiment. Three test cases (12 to 14) are presented in this chapter.

Chapters-7 presents the results obtained for the Three-dimensional path calculation of an Autonomous Underwater Vehicle against a static obstacle. The results obtained are from the respective proposed mathematical protocol, simulator, and experiment. One test case (15) is presented in this chapter. Along with the test case, a proposal on MAUV for an international patent is presented in this chapter.

Chapter-8 analyses the proposed novel mathematical protocols, simulation, and experimentation results and summarizes the work.

Chapter-9 presents the overall conclusions drawn based on the present investigation and proposal for future work.

Chapter 2

Literature Survey

2.1 Meta-analysis of Literature Survey

The research work carried in the field of robot path planning is presented in this section. A detailed metadata analysis of the literature collected is shown in Figures 2.1 to 2.5. Figure 2.1 shows the pie-chart of the literature survey in terms of different sub-topics, whereas Figure 2.2 is a pie-chart of literature type, literature starting from the year 1964 to the current date is collected and presented in Figure 2.3 as a two-dimensional line chart, and Figure 2.4 and 2.5 are Geomap and pie-chart of literature publishing country. Around two hundred and fifty papers from the field of robotics, especially path planning, are surveyed as a part of the literature.

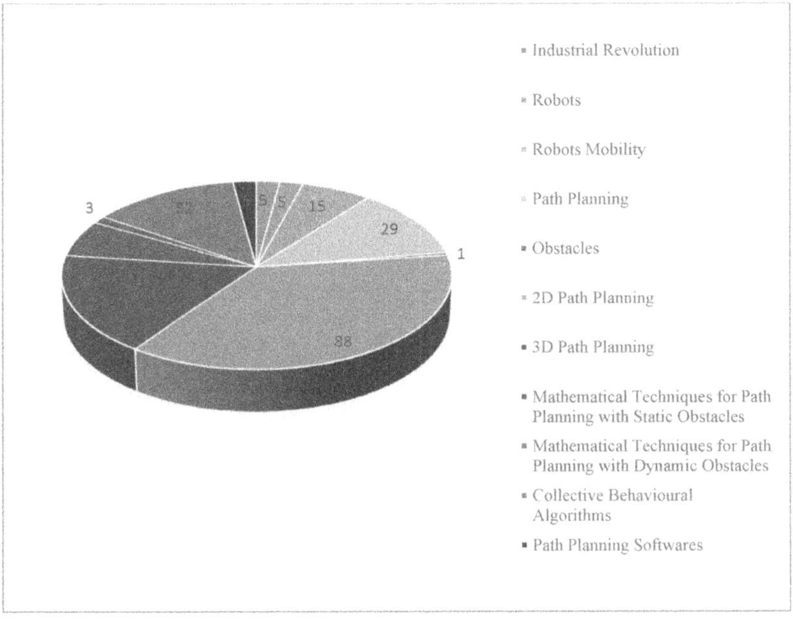

Figure 2.1: Literature Survey – Topic Wise (No.)

2.2 Categorisation of the Literature Survey

In the present work, the literature survey is categorised into five parts i.e.

1. Classical path planning techniques for robots.
2. Reactive path planning techniques for robots.
    a. Bio-inspired reactive path planning techniques.
3. Path planning algorithms.
4. Type of Obstacles
    a. Two-dimensional static obstacles
    b. Two-dimensional dynamic obstacles
5. Experimentation and Simulation

Each group of literature and research gaps identified in individual parts are explained below.

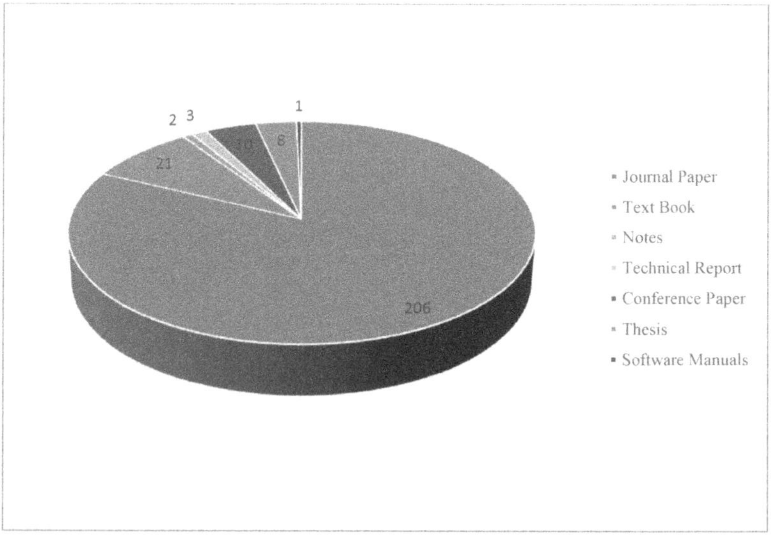

Figure 2.2: Literature Survey – Publication Type (No.)

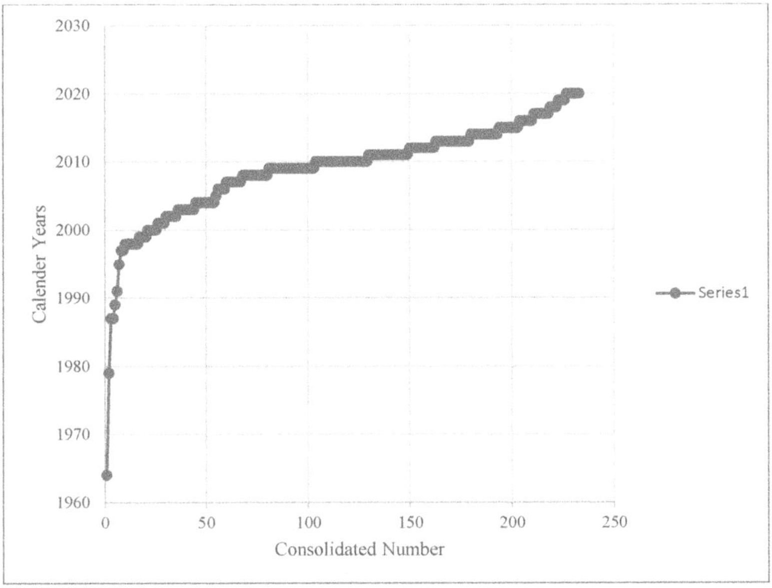

Figure 2.3: Literature Survey – Year Wise (No.)

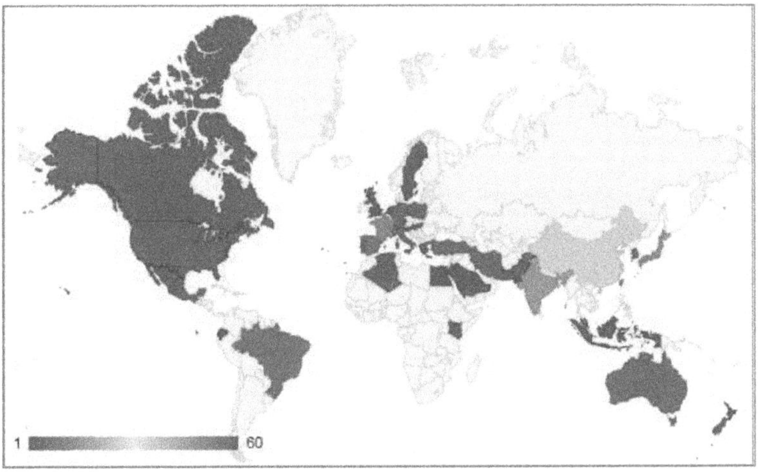

Figure 2.4: Literature Survey – Geomap (No.)

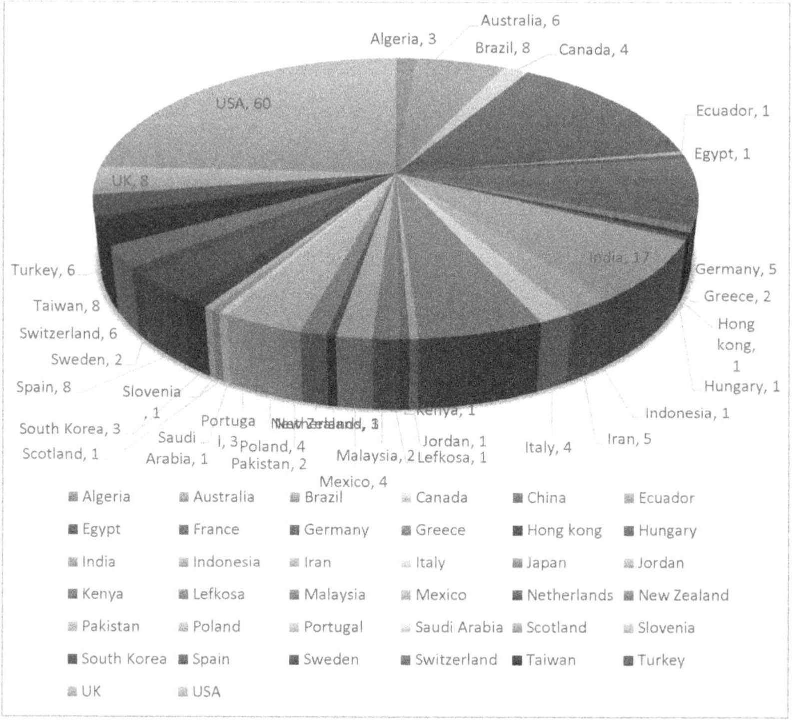

Figure 2.5: Literature Survey - Publishing Country-Wise (No.)

2.2.1 Classical Path Planning Techniques for Robots

Up till now, quite a good number of approaches and methods have been used for the path planning of mobile robots. Patle B K et al. [9] reviewed the classical and reactive path planning techniques. Of all these techniques, the conventional geometry space methods, which include Artificial Potential-Field [38 and 39], Agoraphobic Algorithm [13 to 15], and Vector-Field Histogram [16 and 17], provide the heading angle for the avoidance of obstructions. The Dynamic windows strategy (DWS) technique [18 and 19] was a local velocity-based planner, which calculates the optimum zero-collision velocity for a mobile robot. There was also a method used in [20] called the turning point search algorithm, which finds a point around which the mobile robot turns without bumping into obstacles. On the other hand, several research projects for monitoring the control of a mobile robot with wheels have received attention in the literature [21 to 24].

2.2.1.1 Cell Decomposition (CD)

The Cell decomposition (CD) technique splits the space into no overlapping grids (cells) and uses connectivity charts for moving from one cell to another in order to accomplish the target. The arrangement of pure cells that joins the positions indicates the necessary pathway [24 and 25]. The CD approach was categorised into (i) adaptive, (ii) approximate (iii) exact. In the exact cell decomposition [26 and 27], cells have no particular shape and size; however, they can be found out by the map of the environment, structure, and position of the barrier within it. In the approximate decomposition of cells [28 - 30], the planning space was used to define a regular grid that has a specific shape and size; hence it was easy to implement.

The adaptive decomposition of cells comprises the information present in the free space and follows the basic concept of avoiding free space in the regular decomposition of cells. Noborio H et al. [18] have suggested a quad tree-adaptive decomposition. It divides the environment into large cells, but when the cell in the grid was partially occupied, it divides the cell into four equal parts until it becomes empty. It resolved the problem of planning trajectories for robotic chain platforms and a maze-like environment.

The application of a harmonic function to the breakdown of cells in a C-shaped obstacle environment was expanded [33], whereas [34] set out the strategy for planning the trajectories of mobile robots using CAD information. Garibotto et al. [38] provided an approximate sensor-based cellular decomposition strategy to categorise multiple stationary targets within a complex environment. The developed approach surpasses a static environment with the shortest path and provides full environmental coverage. The same model of cell decomposition by sensors was proposed [39 to 41] to deal with an unknown rectilinear working area for the task of a mobile robot. The authors used the CD approach as well as a laser scanning mechanism to avoid objects in unknown surroundings. The authors outlined a hybrid approach aimed to bridge the gap between theoretical achievements and practical considerations in track planning issues. To save time and money, they created an APF-based precise cell decomposition path planner.

The FL, together with the CD, was provided [48] for real-time operation in an unpredictable environment. A greedy depth-first search method and GA-based cell decomposition technique for manipulator route planning were described [49] to manage several activities at once in a three-dimensional environment. Quantitative investigations on the trajectories using different cell decompositions, graph weights, and waypoint calculation procedures [44 and 45] were conducted. A cell decomposition technique for examining the three-dimensional world was used for an aerial navigation challenge. For directing and controlling the aerial vehicle, fuzzy logic was used with the cell decomposition technique in this approach.

2.2.1.2 Roadmap Approach (RA)

The RA was often referred to as the highway approach. It was the path from one location to another, and the connection between the free spaces was represented by a collection of one-dimensional curves [24]. The visibility graph technique connects the starting and ending positions with map nodes. This approach was also utilised in environments with polygonal impediments, where nodes represent the vertices of the polygon and edges serve as connectors between the nodes.

Another roadmap technique used for robot route planning was the Voronoi diagram [27 and 29]. This approach splits the territory into sub-regions in which all obstacle edges were built using equidistant locations from the adjacent two places on the obstacle's bounds. Kavraki L E et al. [31 to 33] describes the use of the Voronoi diagram in the subject of mobile robot navigation around obstacles. Some enhancements for successful path planning were offered to increase performance and minimise disadvantages such as abrupt bends and lengthy loops in the Voronoi diagram. To achieve path optimal solution, the hybrid technique combines the visibility graph, Voronoi diagram, and potential field methodology. The technique has been observed to fail to get the best path, and the implementation procedure was complex.

Various techniques, such as skeleton maps, were used to produce successful path planning utilising Voronoi diagrams. A combination technique of combining a visibility graph and a Voronoi diagram to find the best path was explained in [34]. Sanchez G et al. [32 and 34] described the use of probability in RA to analyse and develop path planning solutions. However, the technique was inefficient in terms of determining the optimal path length. The authors made a slight modification to the probabilistic roadmap technique to enhance the process of identifying the shortest path (PRM). The technique presented the lazy-collision checking strategy with PRM to address the path planning problem in a real-world environment. An unmanned aerial vehicles navigation in a three-dimensional environment has been clearly demonstrated. The road map technique was provided with a probabilistic formulation to control the flying route in this approach.

2.2.1.3 Artificial Potential Field (APF)

For mobile robot navigation, an artificial potential field (APF) method [38] was used. The objective and impediments, according to the study, operate as charged surfaces, and the combined potential produces an imagined force on the robot. This fictitious force pulls the robot toward the objective and keeps it away from obstacles. To avoid the barrier and reach the goal location, the robot follows the negative gradient. Kim JO et al. [39] describes the use of this technique for mobile robot navigation.

Using APF, a new obstacle avoidance method in an unknown environment was discussed in [40 and 38]. To circumvent a local minimum problem, they employed a harmonic function. Ge SS et al. [41 to 43] has also proposed a solution to the problem of local minimum circumstances. The authors looked at the dynamic characteristics of robot navigation in this study. The authors perform a study of APF in a dynamic context for obstacle avoidance. The APF technique has been improved by employing electrostatic principles [44]. The use of electrostatics aids in the generation of the potential function and the determination of the collision-free path in real-time.

Moving obstacle avoidance was a complex problem in a real-time setting; therefore, [45] created a velocity regulating system to comprehend the location and velocity of the obstacle while attaining the target. The superior potential function and superior repulsive potential function [46 and 47] tackle the identified difficulty in mobile robot navigation using APF techniques such as oscillation and conflicts by avoiding local minima and achieving global optima. The study provided an enhanced version of the APF to reduce oscillation and clashes when the objective is near an obstacle.

2.2.1.4 Grid-Based Method

In a grid-based approach, a grid on configuration space is superimposed, with each configuration being represented by a grid point. A robot is allowed to go from each grid point to a neighbouring lattice focus as long as the line between them is wholly contained inside the grid (tested by collision detection). According to Weigl M et al. [15], including free-space data into these matrices improves both the subsequent execution and shape identification when compared to a point-following calculation using box models.

2.2.1.5 Virtual Impedance Method

Motion smoothness was improved using a Virtual Impedance method for a flexible robot. The authors demonstrated virtual power on a portable robot by using a spring as an impediment and calculating impedance control to maintain the desired separation to avoid snags. The non-contacting impedance restriction was a mechanism that was implemented in the controller conduct control for impact avoidance [64]. It has, however, been included in the movement planning of portable robots [65 to 68].

2.2.1.6 Divide and Conquer Method

Jung Won Kang et al. [50] explored the interaction between the robot and its working environment. They used the divide and conquer approach to address difficulties in order to make the search easier, compress the search space, simplify the work of establishing fitness functions, and obtain a distributed controlling system. They have also demonstrated their findings in an experimental setting. Ryan J Meuth et al. [55] developed a quad tree-based approach for finding the shortest path from a given goal location to any given desired target. Their proposed computation works in a 2-D stationary situation with snags of various forms and a self-governing machine with essentially unbounded dimensions.

2.2.1.7 Literature Gaps Identified

1. Based on the literature survey undertaken, it is revealed that very few studies are carried on classical mathematical techniques for robot path planning. The classical approach is easy to implement, but this approach is often required accurate information about the active navigational environment. The entire world of robotics is

going behind the reactive approaches leaving classical approaches, even for global known environments. Not many new techniques are proposed in recent years. Classical methods have several shortcomings such as computational intensiveness, trapping in local minima, inability to handle maximum uncertainty, demand for precise information about the environment, the requirement of a precise sensing mechanism for real-time navigation, and many more. The unpredictable and unreliable nature of these approaches makes their usage brittle in a real-time environment. The majority of the studies are on reactive techniques for path planning rather than classical mathematical techniques.

2. Most of the techniques focused on local navigation rather than global navigation, even for known environments. The complexity involved in multi obstacle, multi-vehicle operations is missed in the majority of the literature. Very few research papers were published on a dynamic environment compared with a static environment.

3. Most of the papers deal with the subject of single robot systems while leaving a vast gap in coordinated and networked multi-robot systems. An interesting point of view is that despite the significant improvement in the area over the past three decades, minimal works have been reported, especially in multi-robot systems. Most of the papers deal with the subject of single robot systems while leaving a comprehensive collection of areas in coordinated and networked multi-robotics systems that are still open for future works.

2.2.2 Reactive Path Planning Techniques for Robots

Reactive approaches such as genetic algorithm, firefly algorithm, fuzzy logic, particle swarm optimisation, neural network, firefly algorithm, particle swarm optimisation, ant colony optimisation, bacterial foraging optimisation, artificial bee colony, cuckoo search, shuffled frog leaping algorithm, and other miscellaneous algorithms such as harmony search algorithm, invasive weed optimisation, differential evolution, bat algorithm, differential evolution, and other miscellaneous algorithms are developed recently. They have a strong capacity to deal with the unpredictability that exists in their surroundings.

2.2.2.1 Proportional Integral Device Controller (PID)

Nonlinearity and uncertainty are the problems in a non-holonomic system. The trajectory inaccuracy for a wheeled mobile robot has always been created and cannot be removed because of this uncertainty. In this regard, several tracking approaches, such as the Proportional Integral Derive (PID) controller [9], have been presented in the literature. However, when the sensor sensitivity affects this controller, it becomes unstable [10].

2.2.2.2 Developed Turning Point Search Algorithm

The endpoint of the safe free section that leads to the shortest path was determined using a newly designed turning point searching method. The method described in [73] addresses two primary goals: path length and path safety.

The goal of this method was to find the endpoint of a free segment that leads to the shortest path. As a result, if the selected free segment's length exceeds the robot's diameter, the endpoint was deemed a turning point. The drawbacks of this method were that it focuses first on finding the shortest path without contemplating safety and then on guaranteeing safe path navigation, resulting in lengthy and costly calculations and requiring more time for designing an appropriate path for a mobile robot.

2.2.2.3 Genetic Algorithm

The genetic algorithm (GA) was a well-known search-based optimisation technique that was based on Bremermann's discovery of genetics and natural selection in 1958. In 1975, the first time it was used in the field of computer science [49]. For a static environment, [72] proposed an application of GA for the mobile robot navigation issue, only in the presence of a polygonal obstruction the analysis was given through simulation results. In real-time, traditional techniques for searching and optimisation were exceedingly sluggish; therefore, Marti K et al. [87 to 89] proposed a real-time path planner.

GA was a powerful search strategy for an unknown environment that requires very little knowledge about the environment to search efficiently. The authors use this approach to fulfil navigational goals such as path length, smoothness, and obstacle avoidance. In challenging locations, this approach addresses the non-linear environmental problem of navigation for a dead end. They have presented an online training model for obtaining the fittest chromosomal in order to avoid becoming stranded in such situations and to find a way out. Most studies have only used GA to offer navigation in a static environment; however, the authors suggest navigation in the presence of a moving barrier in an uncertain environment.

Many studies have coupled the use of GA with another intelligence algorithm to create a hybrid method, such as GA-F, GA-NN, and GA-PSO, to improve outcomes in robot route planning. One of the problems in robotics is multi-robot route planning. Santos et al. [78] used GA to solve the problem of path planning for numerous mobile robots. He devised a time-efficient coordinating approach for avoiding collisions between many robots in a static environment as part of his research.

The method for multiple goals was illustrated [93] for a static environment, similar to multiple robot route planning. Sun S et al. [80 and 83] addressed the navigation problem for a multi-mobile robot system in a dynamic environment. They have shown that the outcomes can be achieved in the face of both static and dynamic barriers. Many studies have found that the GA has certain drawbacks, such as a sluggish convergence rate, no guarantee of getting the best solution, a time-consuming procedure for determining the parameters for mutation rate and population size, and so on.

The authors offer a modified GA path planner for robot navigation that incorporates a population-based co-evaluation method. The authors showed the optimum simulation results for numerous robot systems in an unfamiliar place by changing the GA in terms of collision avoidance and path optimality. The researchers also offer another modified form of GA for path optimisation. The length of the chromosome is changed in their method to achieve the most remarkable results. The GA method effectively adapts to the environment (known and unknown), as evidenced by its use in the three-dimensional path planning problems of underwater and aerial robots, as well as the two-dimensional path planning issue of a humanoid robot.

Patle BK et al. [77] developed the matrix binary code based genetic algorithm (MGA) in the challenging environment for single and multi-robot systems to cope with the challenge of a moving target. The robot can readily monitor the moving barrier and moving objects in this technique and arrives at the destination in a short amount of time. Michalewicz Z et al. [87 and 89] gave a presentation of missile control based on a mix of the GA method and fuzzy logic. The GA is crucial in the development of the missile's guiding law. The authors provide a unique GA-based approach for military and ocean monitoring applications.

2.2.2.4 Fuzzy Logic (FL)

FL was initially introduced in 1965 and has since been used by all sectors of research and development. Tungal et al. [20, 48 and 63], a fuzzy (Sugeno) based navigation for the omnidirectional mobile robot was given. For successful navigation, an automated fuzzy rule generating method for obstacle avoidance was created. The navigation system was provided in unstructured static and dynamic domains utilising fuzzy logic, which eliminates navigation issues such as continuous looping, backtracking, dead-end traps (U-shaped, labyrinth, snails), steering from restricted passages, and curved trajectory.

Xu J et al. [70 to 73] used FL as a data-driven technique to address navigation issues in a dynamic environment. The authors described a cooperative navigation strategy for numerous mobile robots in a crowded environment and proposed a stereo vision-based mechanism with FL to increase the robot's capacity in a moving state. They devised a Mamdani-based FL controller for a wheeled mobile robot to follow the moving item. To choose the optimal parameters, they used the PSO algorithm with FL in a hybrid method.

Saroj Kumar et al. [84] use fuzzy logic for path planning of airborne robots and underwater robots, respectively, to handle one of the toughest challenges of navigation in a three-dimensional environment. The FL method has been used to control and guide missiles, drones, and underwater robots in the defence industry. The fuzzy logic with PNG (proportional navigation) to produce missile acceleration instructions based on closing velocity and LOS (line-of-sight) rate. A fuzzy group decision support system to choose a suitable UAV (unmanned aerial vehicle) for a military mission was proposed by the authors. By managing both language and conventional quantitative information, fuzzy logic plays an essential part in a multi-criteria decision-making dilemma in his work.

2.2.2.5 Fuzzy Logic Controller

Furthermore, a fuzzy logic controller was employed in [63], although due to the intensive calculation, this control rule has a sluggish reaction time [20]. In other studies, sliding mode controllers were employed in a variety of applications [48 and 71]. This control system's main benefit was that it ensures stability, robustness, quick reaction, and good transient [84].

2.2.2.6 Neural Network (NN)

Artificial Neural Networks (ANNs) were intelligent systems made up of numerous primary and linked processing components. Orozco-Rosas U et al. [48, 63 and 72] demonstrated the use of a NN for navigation of a wheeled mobile robot in a largely unknown environment. Various techniques were combined with the NN as a hybrid mechanism to get the best outcome during a robot navigation operation. Sagiroglu et al. [73 to 76] described how the NN and APF collaborated to achieve cooperative and competitive coordination for behaviour-based control.

Chan et al. [81 and 82] demonstrated the use of the NN in conjunction with sonar for mobile robot navigation. They used ultrasonic sensors to create a real-time neural control system for a mobile robot. They modified the basic NN to develop GAPCNN to obtain quick convergence of parameters for a mobile robot operating in a static and dynamic environment to increase the performance of the NN. It requires minimal statistical training, explores complex relationships between dependent and independent variables, was capable of detecting and solving all possible interactions between predictor variables, and provides multiple training algorithms, and was thus used in the path planning problem of humanoid robots and industrial robots in a two-dimensional environment, underwater robots, and aerial robots. As a result, Bishop CM et al. [78 and 79] suggested using a NN to simulate the nonlinear mapping from many sensor inputs to the optimal output. They demonstrated the use of NN-based pattern classification for target recognition, which has now become commonplace in military equipment.

2.2.2.7 Bio-inspired Reactive Path Planning Techniques

2.2.2.7.1 Firefly Technique (FA)

In 2008, Yang introduced the Firefly Algorithm (FA). Although it was also known as the meta-heuristics algorithm, it was inspired by the flashing characteristic of fireflies. Its approach was based on random states and broad identification, similar to the trial and error method used by fireflies in nature. In the face of a static barrier, Gaussier P et al. [90] proposed an FA-based mobile robot navigational method. They have fulfilled the three primary navigational objectives of path length, smoothness, and safety.

In a simulation setting alone, Soueres P et al. [51, 58, 61, and 91] proposed the FA for the shortest collision-free path for single mobile robot navigation. In three-dimensional marine conditioning, they devised a scheduling approach for swarm robots to minimise interference and jamming. In the same setting, they use the same light-firefly based method to solve another real-world underwater navigation problem in a part known environment. They describe an FA-based cooperative method for detecting dead robots in a multi-mobile robot system.

The study of a Firefly Algorithm (FA) for a single as well as a multi-robot system in the presence of a variety of obstacles (concave, zigzag, and convex) was assessed. Many researchers are doing studies for robot route planning, including an FA-vision-based system, FA-Q learning technique, firefly artificial bee colony (FAABC) hybrid approach, and others. The use of FA to a legged robot and an underwater robot was demonstrated in [44 to 47].

2.2.2.7.2 Particle Swarm Optimization (PSO)

PSO [59] was a bio-inspired meta-heuristic method that replicates the behaviour of fish schools, bird flocks, and other animals. PSO was one of the most widely utilised optimisation strategies for solving engineering, technology, and scientific issues. Using a multi-agent particle filter, [33 and 34] solved the mapping and localisation difficulties of mobile robot navigation in an unfamiliar environment. To solve the dynamic and time-dependent constraint challenges of mobile robot navigation, Siegwart R et al. [53, 56, 107 to 111] developed the Area Extended PSO (AEPSO) as an extension of the original PSO.

Roque Saltaren et al. [105 to 108] investigate the use of PSO to an underwater navigation issue in a complicated three-dimensional environment. The combined PSO-UFastSLAM method was utilised in that study to increase estimation accuracy and restrict the particles for better outcomes. The PSO method has been successfully applied for navigation of an aerial robot in a three-dimensional unknown environment, a humanoid robot, and an industrial robot, similar to underwater robots. They compared different techniques such as GA, PSO, NN, and FL to determine the optimum navigational control, concluding that FL combined with PSO provides the most excellent results in terms of distance travelled. PSO's applicability was not only restricted to mobile robot navigation in the defence industry. The authors proposed the use of PSO for non-deterministic UAV navigation, allowing them to collaborate toward the aim of guarding a large region against aerial attack.

2.2.2.7.3 Ant Colony Optimization (ACO)

Marco Dorigo created this swarm intelligence system in his PhD thesis in 1992. Deepika et al. [52, 54, 57 and 92] presented the use of ACO for real-time path planning of mobile robots. When compared to other algorithms such as GA, the ACO improves convergence speed, solution variation, computing efficiency, and dynamic convergence behaviour. The authors use ACO to show navigation for numerous mobile robots. In a static setting, they demonstrated a collision avoidance technique for several robot systems.

The authors proposed to offer an RA-ACO-based method for humanoid robot navigation in a crowded environment. They used Petri-Net to evaluate the suggested technique for navigation of numerous humanoid robots in a real-time environment and found good agreement between simulation and real-time findings. They propose a change to improve the performance of the current ACO method in the static environment. According to them, convergence speed is the most critical factor in performance.

2.2.2.7.4 Bacterial Foraging Optimization (BFO)

Passino introduced a novel nature-inspired optimisation method based on the behaviour of E. coli and M. Xanthus bacteria in 2002. Montiel Oscar et al. [42 and 48] demonstrate the use of the BFO method for mobile robot navigation in a static environment with changing velocity based on uniform, Gauss, and Cauchy distributions.

In the presence of multiple obstacles, the same strategy was presented in [42 and 63] for static-environment navigation. The authors present real-time navigation in corridor, lobby, and building floor environments for a single mobile robot system.

2.2.2.7.5 Artificial Bee Colony (ABC)

Kharaboga proposes the ABC, a swarm-based intelligent method inspired by the behaviours of honeybees in quest of nourishment. The ABC algorithm was a population-based method comprised of inherent solutions (food source for bees). Shi et al. [45 and 90] propose an application of the ABC algorithm to mobile robot navigation in a static environment. The suggested method employs ABC for local search and an evolutionary algorithm to determine the best path. For result validation, real-time trials in an indoor context are given. They describe a similar technique in a static setting; however, the results were confined to simulation situations. The authors propose an ABC-based strategy to achieve the aim of navigation in a real-time dynamic environment. They suggested a hybridised technique that combined the ABC algorithm with a time rolling window strategy.

2.2.2.7.6 Shuffled Frog Leaping Technique (SFLA)

Eusuff and Lansey created this meta-heuristic optimisation technique based on the behaviour of frogs in search of food. In the realm of engineering optimisation, the SFLA has gained popularity. Valavanis KP et al. [43] created a path planning approach for avoiding a locally optimal solution problem based on the median strategy. They adjusted the fitness algorithm for optimal route creation, resulting in the world's best frog, whose location was utilised to guide the robot's movement in the midst of static and dynamic impediments. The authors showed a multi-objective method based on SFLA to accomplish navigational goals such as path safety, path length, and path smoothness.

2.2.2.8 Literature Gaps Identified

1. There is an evident ambiguity in the size and number of components required for the reactive technique-based path planning. Even though reactive approaches are extra

intellectual and extra innovative as they can acclimate to both uncertain (unknown) and specific environments, to compensate for the incomplete information about the environment, more electronic parts are embedded into the robot system, making it bulkier. Limitation of hardware components is an issue in path planning implementation. Most of the reactive algorithms are not able to provide good results in the real-time path planning problem, which is very clear from the literature surveyed.

2. The arbitrary technique, supported by the rules of bionics, represents a difficulty with respect to the application of scientific techniques, which so much contributed to the technological advancement in the modern world. Mimicking the behaviour of animals or birds is very difficult. As observed from the literature, there are no hypothetical procedures for bionics.
3. There are many fewer papers on hybrid algorithms compared with those on standalone algorithms. Path planning techniques are not heuristic; getting close to the actual solution needs a mixed approach. The performance of classical approaches can be improved by hybridising with reactive approaches. Customisation is lacking in robot path planning.
4. In a dynamic environment, there are many fewer papers on the navigation of a robot for a moving goal problem compared with a moving obstacle problem. There are many classical and reactive path planning algorithms for a dynamic environment, but most of them are confined only to simulation, and very few of them are used in real-time experimentation.

2.2.3 Path Planning Algorithms

2.2.3.1 CD and AI Algorithms

Seda Milos et al. [13] addressed the concept of dividing large learning environments into numerous smaller ones to facilitate exploration. The Cell Decomposition (CD) approach is widely utilised in path planning issues in the literature. Global path planning employing optimisation algorithms was referred to as the AI direction. As noted by Batsaikhan et al. [19 - 22], AI-based techniques provide complicated computing and are more trustworthy when the environmental information was unclear. The fuzzy techniques used relative location and velocity between the robot and the goal, as well as the robot and the obstacle, as inputs and outperformed previous potential field methods.

2.2.3.2 Multipoint Potential Field Algorithm

In an obstacle avoidance issue, Castillo O et al. [93] used multipoint PF. The roadmap was made up of a series of pathways, each of which is made up of collision-free area connections. The built network, a roadmap will be used for motion planning.

2.2.3.3 Path Search Algorithm

The route search algorithm was a method that looks for the path between the starting point and the end using an existing environment model [95 and 97]. To get an ideal trajectory to link two places while fulfilling various sorts of restrictions, such as avoiding obstacles and objects, a minimal turning radius, maximum acceleration, maximum energy consumption, and low time consumption, a trustworthy and effective algorithm is required. The AUV path search algorithm has yielded fruitful results and has been widely applied; factors to consider in an AUV path search algorithm include environmental uncertainty and dynamic characteristics, real-time, the validity and optimality of the planning algorithm, and satisfying the constraints of the robot body's ability to move.

The primary reason for this was that as the robot's functional space was expanded to three-dimensional, the kinematics and dynamics restrictions become extremely complicated [98]. The advantages and disadvantages of two-dimensional and three-dimensional path search methods used on AUVs are examined and contrasted, and better algorithms are devised. The algorithm's real-time performance, optimal performance, and dependency on the environment model were also compared, and references were supplied for future in-depth research.

2.2.3.4 Geometrical Method Algorithms

Geometric model search methods were traditional route search techniques that fall under the umbrella of discrete optimum programming. This section of the algorithm was more conventional; the implementation method was straightforward, the technology was quite established, and the model establishment was extremely rigorous, which was directly connected to the outcomes of the final planning route implementation. The concept behind the sub-goal approach was to address the mobility planning problem by using a list of possible configurations from the beginning place. Several researchers used sub-networks in route and robot motion planning issues. The authors proposed a sub-network variant based on hierarchical path search. To find a path that was free of obstacles for convex static polygons for a point robot. Raju [35] suggested a technique called Sloping Line Search (SLS). Ravindranadh [37] suggested an innovative approach. Coordinate Reference Frame for a point robot to avoid convex and concave polygonal obstacles.

With weighted digraphs or undirected graphs, Dijkstra's algorithm uses a greedy strategy that employs a breadth-first search to resolve the single-source shortest path issue; it declares an array to hold the shortest distance from the source point to each vertex and saves while finding the set of vertices for the shortest path; the algorithm eventually obtains a shortest-path tree. Dijkstra's method was used to a global path search for AUVs in an underwater environment by Sfeir et al. [46 to 48 and 64], and the algorithm was able to avoid a series of obstacles and reach the end. The experiment, however, was just in the simulation stage and did not take into account the influence of the environment on path search; the next step will be to undertake experimental verification in the tank.

2.2.3.5 Algorithms for AUVs

The selection of the evaluation function f (n) in the A* algorithm is critical, and the evaluation function is linked to the planning of the AUV's shortest and optimal path [11]. The A* algorithm has the benefit of being able to be halted and recovered in time throughout the planning process, resulting in a heuristic path with a low cost and optimum solution. The A* algorithm's function and benefits in the path search job of the AUV underwater complicated environment are demonstrated in [69]. Sagiroglu et al. [73 to 74] used the A* algorithm to create a route search that reflects the effect of marine environmental variables such as ocean currents. To improve processing performance, the authors applied a hierarchical approach to the A* algorithm.

AUV three-dimensional path planning [74] and vehicle routing [75] were solved using a modified SFLA method for mobile robot navigation. The authors developed an SFLA-based flight control technique for air-breathing hypersonic vehicles for defence purposes. A modified SFLA using the proportional integral derivative technique was developed for the climb, cruise, and descent flight control, comprising the height loop, pitch angle loop, and velocity loop.

Yinjing Guo et al. [11] ignore water depth across a wide variety of underwater settings, simplifying a three-dimensional space to a two-dimensional underwater environment model based on the grid technique for an AUV. Despite the loss of environmental data, the system saves space and produces good results.

A recursion of free space into many subspaces was called an octree model, and the resulting subspace can have three states: free subspace, obstacle subspace, and mixed subspace [24 and 25]. The octree model was used to simulate a real underwater environment. This approach, however, has three significant flaws. The spatial neighbourhood of each block was challenging to specify since the initial space (or picture) was changed in the tree data structure. Second, because the AUV routes created by the octree are confined to the portions between the block centres, they are suboptimal. They utilise an octomap to zoom in and out as needed, and article [31] goes through the octomap for an AUV in greater depth. The authors use the open-source framework to modify and design a collision-free course for AUV in an unknown environment if a nearby impediment is detected during the mission.

An irregular grid terrain system for an AUV portrays an underwater environment with irregular graphics; the shape of the graphics is determined by the undersea topography [35]. The modelling was more sophisticated and took up a lot of space when compared to a conventional grid terrain model. However, it has an excellent storage efficiency and can adequately represent the structural characteristics of the seafloor landscape. This model can handle a vast amount of terrain data, was simple to update, and has varying resolution depending on the geometry of the seabed topography, allowing for terrain simplification [47].

The Voronoi diagram, also referred to as the Thiessen polygon or Dirichlet diagram, was made up of a sequence of uninterrupted polygons made up of vertical bisectors connecting two neighbours' straight lines [42]. A Voronoi graph's vertices belong to three Voronoi polygons at the same time, and each Voronoi polygon has only one node. This approach can hold a significant amount of data for a complicated terrain, is useful when examining the topography of the seafloor, and can make the terrain simpler. The most significant benefit of Voronoi diagram-based environment modelling was that the path in the road map was the Voronoi edge, which was the mid-perpendicular to the discrete centre of an obstruction, ensuring that the AUV was kept far away from impediments throughout operations [38].

However, there was a vast amount of data to store, and the path length was not always ideal. In a two-dimensional Voronoi diagram, [18] indicated the position of an obstacle and used the Voronoi processor to construct an estimated path connecting the origin and goals. The Voronoi map was widely used in three-dimensional model creation compared to two-dimensional space. The authors use a three-dimensional Voronoi diagram to build a global route, which was a typical modelling approach for ensuring a safe path for an AUV.

Borenstein J et al. [40 and 43] offer some instances of subsurface modelling for AUVs utilising Voronoi diagrams. The Voronoi diagram has the benefit of generating a path that is generally safe and far away from obstacles, and the path search is done on curves or surfaces; nevertheless, the resulting path is not remarkably smooth. The authors included a Fermat spiral segment based on the Voronoi diagram model and developed a curvature continual model-building technique for an AUV in response to this challenge; the Fermat spiral is utilised to smooth the path and give curvature.

The Delaunay triangle was a one-to-one relationship between the Voronoi diagram and the three-node Voronoi polygon that links three concurrent nodes. As a result, this model has the same benefits and drawbacks as the Voronoi diagram model. When the obstacle evolves, the modelling technique based on the Delaunay triangle model simply needs to modify the vertex parameters of the storage edge, and the triangulation network does not need to be rebuilt. Delaunay triangulation empty circle characteristics and minimum angle maximisation properties, as a reciprocal Voronoi graph, guarantee that no Delaunay triangulation emerges in a triangle that was too slender and narrow, making triangulation construction more reasonable and accurate because it maximises the minimum inner angle of all triangulations [46]. As a result, this model has been used widely in the path planning of AUVs in map construction.

Sfeir J et al. [46 and 47] created an enhanced triangulation growth method for an AUV that combines the notion in the divide-and-conquer algorithm. It increases the baseline using the regional discrimination concept of linear equations and looks for the third point using the minor cosine criteria, resulting in realistic three-dimensional seafloor terrain vector modelling based on data from a sea trial measurement.

Yan et al. [33 and 51] used the c-space approach to real-world AUV route planning experiments. They suggested an enhanced visibility graph space model for an AUV that decreases the number of constructing nodes to achieve a quick computation time. Based on this data, the spiral algorithm was introduced to improve obstacle avoidance. The visibility graph model has the benefit of being intuitive: the shortest path may be clearly determined. The drawback is that if the beginning and goal locations change, the view must be rebuilt, resulting in a lack of flexibility. This approach has limited local path planning capacity and is best suited for global path planning and trajectory planning in the continuous domain [38 and 39].

2.2.3.6 Literature Gaps Identified

1. A small number of classical techniques are proposed in the last decade for two-dimensional planar robots avoiding static obstacles. Classical techniques available are not compared against experimental results.
2. The availability of literature is significantly less on underwater robots. Both classical and reactive algorithms available for underwater robot path planning are limited in contrast to aerial robots. A considerable gap in the research of modular underwater robots is a big challenge for underwater exploration and maintenance. As per the survey, no research is available to provide a good depth range, working time, and

behavioural capabilities of oceans to match mission requirements across a spectrum of tasks.

3. Very few papers are available in the field of non-linear responses of underwater vehicles. Research is adequate regarding the sea dynamics and unpredictable behaviours.

2.2.4 Review based on Types of Obstacles

2.2.4.1 Two-dimensional Static Obstacles

Earlier research treated the obstacle as a prohibited zone in an outdoor setting and attempted to identify the shortest path from the starting point to the target position. For several distance standards, Ravindranath [97] established computer algorithms for calculating the shortest distance between two locations in a plane. Singh et al. [98] expanded on the previous work by looking at single and two polygonal prohibited areas with just convex polygons.

When the path was constrained by two circular prohibited zones, Seshasayee [99] attempted to determine the minimum Euclidean distance between the source and destination. In the presence of both convex and non-convex polygonal obstacles, Raju [35] developed a geometric methodology known as the SLS technique to identify all the obstacle-free routes.

Viswa Mohan [36] went on to extend this work to discover solutions to three convex and non-convex polygons, which he used for mobile robot path planning. The aforementioned techniques scan all vertices for obstacle-free routes, which takes a long time to compute. Ravindranadh's CRF method [37] solves the limitations described in [97 and 98].

2.2.4.2 Two-dimensional Dynamic Obstacles

Kant et al. [100 to 102] investigated the situation in which several moving obstacles' space-time trajectories are known. They have presented a methodology that generates a viable path given known velocities and trajectories. When the method was implemented identically on many robots, the authors developed a virtual impedance-based strategy that allows a collision-free path to the desired target configuration. In addition, motion planning in dynamic settings was handled by including a time dimension in the robot's configuration space with known obstacle trajectories and assuming limited velocities.

By exploring a visibility graph in the configuration-time space, Reif et al. [103] found a solution to the planar issue for a polygonal robot amid numerous moving polygonal obstacles. Erdmann et al. [104] used a discretized configuration space to sequence slices of the configuration space at different time intervals for robot-assisted assembly activities. At each slice, this approach solves the static planning issue and connects neighbouring solutions. Ravindranadh [37] devised a method for determining the best path for two or three robots in a time-varying environment, based on the first robot's location and the second and third robots' accessible cones.

2.2.4.3 Literature Gaps Identified

1. The geometrical/mathematical techniques developed for a point robot traversing in a planar environment with static obstacles is limited to polygons. Literature is adequate to know about how the robot reacts to curvature obstacles like circles and or ellipses.
2. The classical techniques available in the literature for a planar robot moving in an environment avoiding dynamic obstacles is confined to simulation. No comparative performance study for the proposed algorithm with real-time experimentation is available.

2.2.5 Experimentation and Simulation

Locomotion was the primary issue, which has an impact on mobile robot fabrication. To model the kinematics and dynamics of the robot, it was essential to have a clear idea of the type and number of wheels [85]. In general, traction and stability, manoeuvrability, and control are primary issues under the focus [86 and 87].

Three wheels are adequate for maintaining balance; however, two-wheeled robots can also be stable [88, 90]. The authors suggest that there are additional wheel variations. Walking robots also have the benefit of being able to cope with hurdles or fissures in the surroundings [85], in other words, flexibility and agility over rugged terrain. Robots utilizing treads or caterpillar tracks instead of wheels were characterized as tracked robots. The first assumption is that wheels cannot slide against the surface in the wheel arrangements. Another steering option, known as skid/slip, employs spinning wheels in the same direction at different speeds or in reverse directions to redirect the robot. In comparison to classic wheeled robots, tracked robots have significantly bigger ground contact patches, which helps to enhance their handling on loose terrain.

Castillo O et al. [93] presented a tiny subsurface robot for the maritime observation that was ideal for a fixed point or limited range and subsurface slit and gully areas of ocean monitoring.

An autonomous mobile robot's ability to learn about its work environment and itself is significant. This was accomplished by using sensors and then extracting valuable data from the sensor's readings. The integration of sensors allows robot positioning and localization to be accomplished [94]. They are also utilised for representation and mapping [95]. They are also highly beneficial in other robotic applications like object identification [96 and 97].

A mobile robot's mechanical design must be regulated in order for it to execute tasks and achieve its goals. Perception, processing and cognition, and action are the three pillars of the controller design. Characteristics such as local stability, bifurcation of fixed points, phase diagrams, isoclines, attractors, and others can be used to define the control system.

Azali Saudi et al. [63] implemented the ROBOPATH simulation programme to assess the APF's applicability. For diverse environmental circumstances, several mobile robots are examined, and they reported improved outcomes in coordinating strategy without collisions. Many approaches, such as BFO, GA, PSO, and FL, are utilized to boost the effectiveness of the APF path planner.

2.2.5.1 Literature Gaps Identified

1. Most of the experimentation methodologies mentioned in the literature are confined to an embedded system-based approach. Path planning techniques required for the robot's mobility is given the least priority.

2. Very few simulators are available for testing robot path planning. No open-source simulator is available to compare classical and reactive path planning techniques. Most of the available simulators are closed source. The availability of literature is minimal on simulators and their limitations. Very little, to the extent of single-digit number simulators, are available for underwater robot path planning.

2.3 Shortcomings based on the Literature Gaps Identified

1. Quoting several shortcomings like computational intensiveness, trapping in local minima, inability to handle maximum uncertainty, demand for precise information about the environment, the requirement of a precise sensing mechanism for real-time navigation, the unpredictable and unreliable nature of the Classical methods, less research reported in the last two decades. The majority of the studies are on reactive techniques for path planning rather than classical mathematical techniques. Fewer mathematical techniques were developed last decade. Most of the protocols focused on local navigation rather than global navigation, even for known environments. Based on the literature survey undertaken, it is revealed that very few studies are carried on classical mathematical techniques for robot path planning.

2. Very few research papers are published based on a dynamic environment compared with a static environment. Limited classical techniques are developed for a dynamic environment in the last decade. Few classical path planning algorithms developed earlier for a dynamic environment are majorly confined only to simulation, and very few of them are used in real-time experimentation. No comparative study was reported between classical algorithms and reactive algorithms in a dynamic environment.

3. The availability of the literature is less on AUVs. A small number of classical and reactive algorithms are available for underwater robot path planning in contrast to aerial robots. The literature emphasizes the use of single-unit fixed AUVs underwater, a lot of which fail because of their complex construction.

4. Not a lot of simulators in the market for robotic path planning are available. Most of them are closed source. The availability of literature is minimal on the pros and cons of the simulators, and a trickle of application software is available for underwater

robot path planning. One or two articles show the comparative study of robotic path planning among algorithm application, experimentation, and simulation.

The objective and methodology adopted for the present investigation are derived thoroughly from the literature reviewed. Summarized below are the research gaps identified from the literature to carry out the present investigation.

2.4 The Objective of the Work-Based on Gaps in Literature

1. The objective of the present work is to develop few novel mathematical (classical) protocols to study the obstacle avoidance path planning of a robot. In a two-dimensional planar arena, for the robot to take the path avoiding elliptical and or circular obstacles, a new mathematical protocol, and for mixed elliptical and polygonal obstacles, together with Coordinate Reference Frame (CRF), is used. These classical protocols are intended to address the global navigation issue. Against few arbitrary test cases, results are calculated and compared against reactive based experimental results and simulation results.

2. The current investigation answers the shortcoming regarding the efficiency of mathematical techniques in two-dimensional dynamic path planning. A time-based protocol, Minimum Path Deviation (MPD), is used, which works using the position information of the first robot and reachable cone of the second to determine possible collisions at a future time and thus in a position to avoid them by deviating from the nominal path. To compare the results of the classical technique MPD protocol, a Particle Swarm Optimization (PSO) technique-based embedded system (reactive based) experimental setup is established for two similar robots which are crossing each other. The robots communicate with each other mimicking this PSO reactive technique.

3. For a three-dimensional environment, a mathematical (classical) protocol is presented, which divides the underwater obstacles into a number of planes to find out the plane with the most significant area. The robot traverse depth up to this plane, from where it uses a two-dimensional path planning technique to move across the obstacles and moves down to the destination. The primary protocol, which calls all

the above-said sub-protocols, is coded using MATLAB®. Design for a modular underwater vehicle system is proposed in the present research.

4. To use existing application software to simulate paths of robots for all two-dimensional, three-dimensional, and dynamic test cases. The results of the simulator are compared with the results of classical mathematical protocols and reactive experimental results.

Chapter 3

Methodology

This chapter deals with the details of the methodologies developed, adopted and tested to investigate and compare the path planning techniques.

In this thesis, three different methodologies are implemented. They are,

1) Mathematical Protocols
2) Experimental Procedures
3) Simulation Procedures

3.1 Mathematical Protocols

This section discusses the mathematical protocols for generating anti-collision paths for mobile robots. In the most basic form, trajectory planning can be dealt with as a purely geometrical problem; compute a robot's collision-free trajectory between two specified locations, taking into account the geometry of the robot and the obstacles. Computational geometry principles are used to design paths for moving robots that avoid collision with static and dynamic obstacles. Computational geometry refers to the study of practical algorithms for solving geometric problems. Computational geometry methodologies make it possible to design and analyse algorithms to effectively solve many geometrical problems which arise in application fields such as manufacturing, computer-aided design, robotics, computer vision and graphics.

3.1.1 Boundary Conditions

3.1.1.1 Constrained and Un-constrained Path

If the obstacles are not present in the Euclidean path between the robot's starting point and endpoint, the path is free, and no distinct procedure is required. Nevertheless, if the obstacles are in the way, joining the starting and the endpoints, then computation of feasible alternate paths are necessary. Figure 3.1 shows Un-constrained and constrained paths.

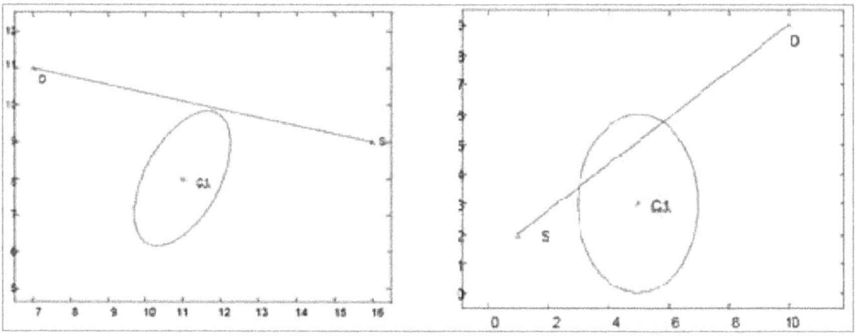

Figure 3.1: Graphical representation of unconstrained and constrained paths in the presence of a single elliptical obstacle, respectively

3.1.1.2 Configuration Space

The design of "configuration space" [37 and 110] makes trajectory planning analysis much more straightforward. The robot is depicted as a dot, known as a configuration, in a space set up encoding the degree of freedom of the robot in the configuration space. Barriers in the workspace map prevent access to the setup space. Supplementing these regions is "open space". Designing the trajectory of any size robot can therefore reduce the problem of trajectory planning for a point robot in this open space.

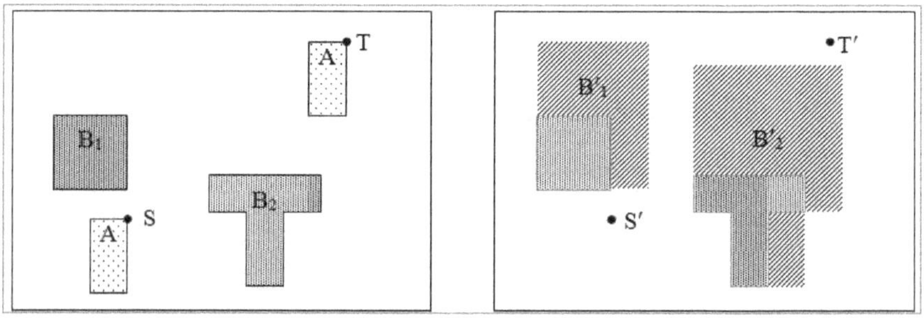

a. Robot A, Obstacles B_1, B_2 in Original Space b. Point Robot at S′ and Obstacles B'_1 B'_2

Figure 3.2: Configuration Space

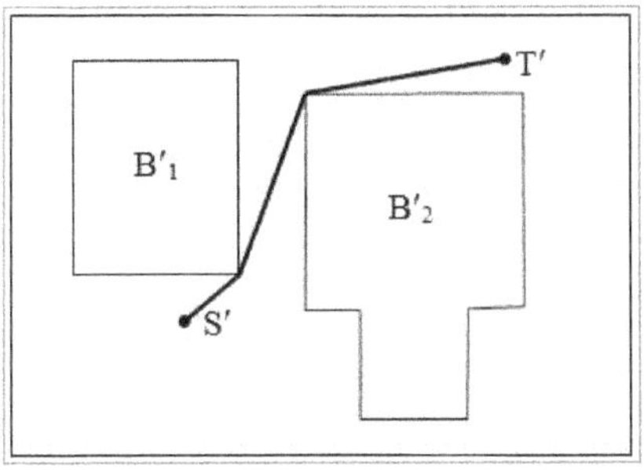

Figure 3.3: Path of robot

A mobile robot is represented by rectangle A, and the obstacles are represented by B_1 and B_2, as shown in Figure 3.2a. A point S is taken somewhere on the mobile robot (the top right corner is considered in this case). Then, to convert to configuration space, one can shrink the mobile part to a reference point S′ representing point robot while simultaneously growing the obstacles B_1, B_2 to B'_1 and B'_2 respectively as shown in Figure 3.2b by sliding rectangle A along the boundaries of obstacles. As long as the referential point S′ of rectangle A stays outside the configuration space of obstacles B'_1 and B'_2, rectangle A will not collide with obstacles B_1 and B_2. Thus, the difficulty of finding a path for a rectangular robot is converted into the equivalent problem of finding S′point's path.

Now, the path of the robot is found by finding the collision-free path of the point robot in the free space from reference point S′ to the endpoint T′ in the presence of configuration space obstacles B'_1 and B'_2 as shown in Figure 3.3.

Another valid proposition presented by Lozano Perez et al. [111] in finding the shortest path is: "As long as the mobile part A does not rotate, the shortest path from the reference point (also called starting point) 'S' to the endpoint 'T' is a piecewise-linear path whose breakpoints are vertices of the configuration-space obstacles B'_1 and B'_2 induced by A".

The objective of robot motion planning is to automatically guide a robot around in an environment having obstacles. Economic considerations often mandate the use of a cost function on the robot motion, such as time duration or distance travelled. The shortest path problem is the most accessible instance of a minimum cost path planning issue.

A mobile robot must navigate from a start configuration to an end configuration to perform its task in the given working environment. It will often encounter some restricted areas through which a passage is not permitted or feasible; such areas are called obstacles. Generally, these obstacles represent areas such as ponds, hills, fields etc., in the case of outdoor environments, existing machines, processing areas, tool rooms etc., in the case of indoor environments like industries.

3.1.2 Novel Mathematical Protocols

3.1.2.1 CCT Protocol

Curvature and Common Tangent (CCT) technique is based on finding common tangents between given ellipses and summing them with the line and curvature paths to find the obstacle-free path for moving robot around one or more than one elliptical obstacle.

In the CCT protocol, the rigid obstacle objects are considered elliptical; there might be a single, two or three elliptical or circular obstacle, thus leading to various possible obstacle-free paths. The feasible number of obstacle-free paths will depend upon the number of obstacles, their shape, size, orientation and position. Hence to obtain the possible number of paths, to identify their distances, and to find the shortest among them, a mathematical protocol has been developed.

3.1.2.1.1 Path Planning of Mobile Robot in the Presence of Single Elliptical Obstacle

In this present section, the problem of alternate feasible but dissimilar path generation between a starting point and an endpoint has been attempted. The mobile robot has to move, is containing obstacles; several obstacle-free paths are possible for reaching the endpoint from the starting point. Therefore, in order to reach the endpoint in the shortest possible time, the robot has to choose the shortest path. This necessitates the systematic exploration of all the possible paths connecting the starting point to the endpoint avoiding the obstacles so that an optimum path among these alternatives can be selected. The enumeration of the possible shortest constrained / un-constrained pathways in the presence of a single elliptical obstacle has been given below.

1. Unconstrained
2. Constrained with the region

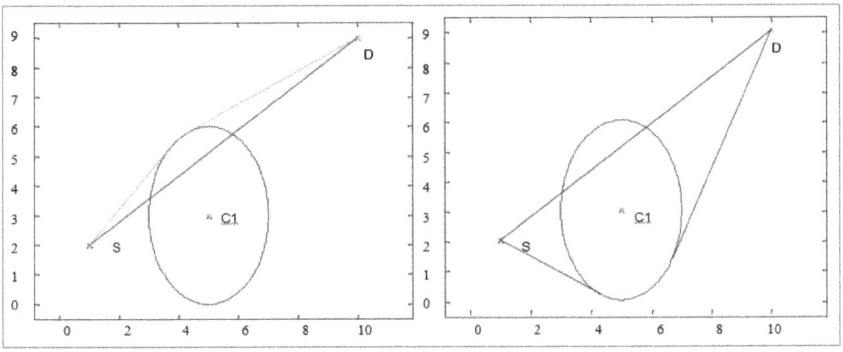

Figure 3.4: Left and Right paths around a single elliptical obstacle

In Section 3.1.1.1, the conditions under which a given path between start and endpoint can be constrained or un-constrained have been enumerated through Figure 3.1, and the objective criterion has been spelt out under enumeration. Understandably, two possible shortest (other combinations are not examined since they are clearly not the best options), yet dissimilar, paths connect the starting point and the endpoint circumventing a single elliptical obstacle as shown in Figure 3.4. To compute the path distances and determine the routes, the method of drawing a pair of tangents from a point to an ellipse whose co-ordinate are known made use of. This yields four points of intersection of tangency from both starting point and endpoint.

Subsequently, using the concept of the location of a point with respect to a line, i.e. to the left or right, the points of tangency are grouped as either left or right. The angle subtended by the radial lines connecting the centre of the ellipse with that of the left pair and right pair of tangency points is then computed. Further, some of the distances of lengths of tangents falling on the same side of the path added to the arc length on the same side of the path gives the total distance function to the left as well as the right of the constrained path SD.

3.1.2.1.2. Path Planning of Mobile Robot in The Presence of Two Elliptical Obstacles

The criteria and means adopted in obtaining alternate paths between the starting point and endpoint in the presence of a single elliptical region have been discussed in the previous section. In this section, the same has been extended to situations wherein the obstacles have been taken to be two. Under the conditions of completely constrained situations, there exist four possible alternate paths between a starting point and an endpoint (other combinations are not examined since they are clearly not the best options). The methods and means that are developed to compute the above paths have been discussed in the following section.

The case of a fully constrained situation (path constrained with both barriers) involves four feasible alternate paths that circumvent two barriers. Computation of the same is done by obtaining the following points of intersection of tangents

a) From the starting point to the first obstacle

b) From the endpoint to the second obstacle

c) Common tangents, on either side, to both the elliptical obstacles

d) Cross tangents between both the obstacles

In accordance with the organisation of the environment, i.e. starting point, endpoint and the obstacles (two ellipses), there are up to four possible alternatives. The solutions are obtained via mathematical expressions.

For obtaining the common tangents between the ellipses, the following mathematical operations are performed.

As known, the general form of an ellipse with centre (h, k) is:

$$\frac{(x-h)^2}{a^2} + \frac{(y-k)^2}{b^2} = 1 \qquad (1)$$

Where a, b are semi-major and semi-minor axes, respectively.

As two ellipses are considered there centres are (h_1, k_1) and (h_2, k_2) with major and minor axes as (a_1, b_1) and (a_2, b_2) in the first and second ellipses, respectively. The product of the rotary matrix with the elliptic equation obtains the orientation of the elliptical shape. The equation of a straight line is in the form of

$$y = mx + c \qquad (2)$$

Where m is the slope and c is a y-intercept

For obtaining a common tangent for the ellipses, equate the slope of the tangent of ellipse 1 to the slope of the tangent of ellipse 2, i.e. (m1=m2). On solving it, a polynomial expression was developed to find the common tangent m' slope between both ellipses by means of the equations 1 and 2, which are given as:

$$Am^4 + Bm^3 + Cm^2 + Dm + E = 0 \qquad (3)$$

The value of m is determined by this expression. As this is an expression in the fourth degree, the slope m has four values that are the slopes of the four possible paths between the two ellipses. Through graphics and simple mathematics, the above points of intersection can be computed. Subsequently, the following four paths can be identified depending on which side of the constrained path a particular path segment lies.

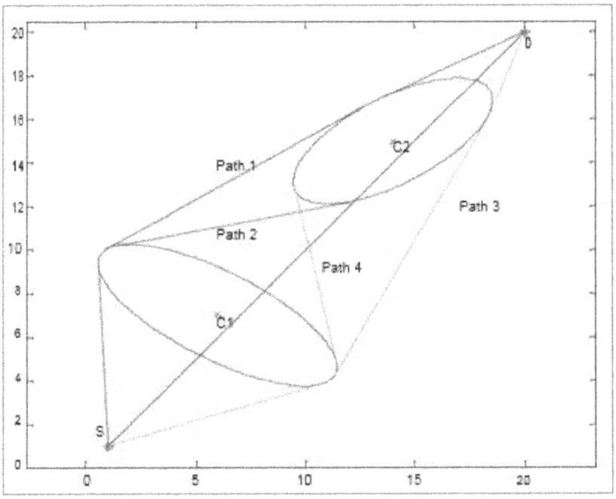

Left-Left (Path 1), Left-Right (Path 2), Right-Right (Path 3), Right-Left (Path 4)

Figure 3.5: All Four possible paths between Two Ellipses

For each of the paths mentioned above, four points of intersection of tangency along with starting point and endpoint form a path. All four possible paths are shown in

Figure 3.5. Computation of distance function is carried out after grouping all those points' pathwise, using simple mathematics. The flowchart for the protocol is shown in Figure 3.6.

3.1.2.1.2.1 CCT Algorithm for Two Elliptical Obstacles

Step 1: Start

Step 2: Input the coordinates of the centre of the ellipse regions and their major and minor axes, angle of orientations.

Step 3: Input the starting point coordinates S (Sx, Sy).

Step 4: Input the endpoint coordinates D (Dx, Dy).

Step 5: Check the type of constraint:

If not constrained with any region, then go to step 6

Else If constrained with a single region, then go to step 7

Else If constrained with two regions, then go to step 8

Step 6: Find the un-constrained direct Euclidean path distance between the starting point S (Sx, Sy) and endpoint D (Dx, Dy) as $d = \sqrt{\{(S_x \sim D_x)^2 + (S_y \sim D_y)^2\}}$, Go to step 9

Step 7: Identify the region with which the direct path from starting point to the endpoint is constrained.

7.1 Apply the technique as discussed in section 4.2.3 with respect to the constrained region, which yields two obstacle-free paths with respect to the current obstacle.

7.2 Check if any of the above two paths are constrained by other obstacles. If so, go to Step 7.4, else go to Step 7.3

7.3 Calculate the path lengths and store the path points coordinates and length of each path in the results file. Go to step 7.9

7.4 Apply the technique and obtain obstacle-free subpaths

7.5 Join these subpaths with the main path

7.6 Calculate the lengths of the paths and store the path points and length of each path in the results file

7.7 Check if the second main path is also constrained by the second obstacle. If so, repeat the steps 7.4 to 7.6; else go to Step 7.9

7.8 Read the paths data from the results file and arrange the paths in the increasing value of the path lengths

7.9 The first path in the revised results file now gives the shortest obstacle-free path between the starting point and endpoint. The other paths in the file provide alternate feasible obstacle-free paths with lengths in increasing order, which are more than the optimum value. Go to step 9.

Step 8: Number the two constrained regions with respect to their distance from the starting point. The nearest one is the first region, and the farthest one is the second region. Go to 8.1

8.1 Apply the technique with respect to the two constrained regions.

8.2 Calculate the path lengths and store the path points, coordinates and length of each path in the results file.

8.3 Read the paths data from the results file and arrange the paths in the increasing value of the path lengths.

8.4 The first path in the revised results file now gives the shortest obstacle-free path between the starting point and endpoint. The other paths in the file provide alternate feasible obstacle-free paths with lengths in increasing order, which are more than the optimum value. Go to step 9.

Step 9: Stop.

3.1.2.1.3 Path Planning of Mobile Robots in the Presence of Three Elliptical Obstacles

The methodology reported for the cases of single elliptical and two elliptical barrier problems has been extended to the case of three elliptical barrier problems. In the present section, an attempt is made to develop a methodology that yields alternate obstacle-free paths to problems involving three elliptical barriers.

The library of alternate obstacle-free paths between a starting point and an endpoint in the presence of barriers to travel will be of immense help for solving routing problems. Therefore, the constrained environment has been thoroughly investigated for all possible geometric conditions. The same has been furnished in the following sections.

Under a fully constrained situation, three elliptical barrier regions form a path between a starting point and an endpoint amount to eight feasible alternate and different routes. As shown in Figure 3.7, these paths are designated below with respect to the path joining starting to the end (other combinations are not examined since they are clearly not the best options).

a) Right-Right-Right path b) Right-Right-Left path c) Right-Left-Right path

d) Right-Left-Left path e) Left-Left-Left path f) Left-Left-Right path

g) Left-Right-Right path h) Left-Right-Left path

The methodology of tangency points and direction selection used in two elliptical barrier region problems has been extended to three elliptical barrier region problems. The following section presents a detailed algorithm along with a flow chart (Figures 3.8 to 3.10). Several problems are solved to evaluate the efficacy of the methodology.

3.1.2.1.3.1 CCT Algorithm for Three Elliptical Obstacles

Step 1: Start

Step 2: Input the coordinates of the centre of the elliptical regions and their major and minor axes and orientation of ellipses.

Step 3: Input the starting point coordinates S (Sx, Sy).

Step 4: Input the endpoint coordinates D (Dx, Dy).

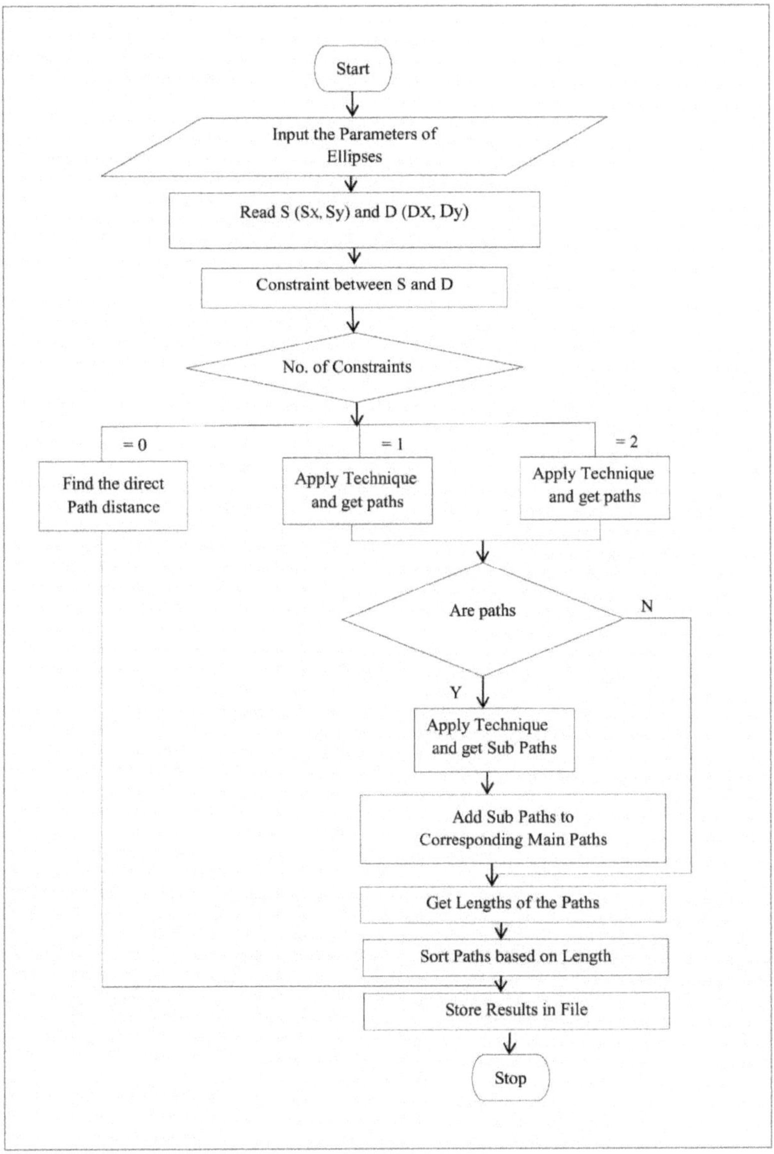

Figure 3.6: CCT Flowchart for Two Elliptical Obstacles

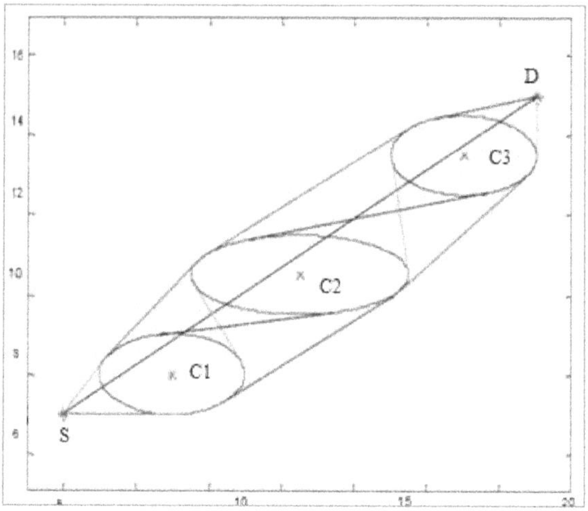

Figure 3.7: Graphical display of alternate Un-constrained Paths in the presence of Three Elliptical Obstacles

Step 5: Check the type of constraint:

If not constrained with any region, then go to step 6

Else if constrained with a single region, then go to step 7

Else if constrained with two regions, then go to step 8

Else (Constrained with three regions) go to step 9

Step 6: Find the un-constrained direct Euclidean path distance between the starting point S (Sx, Sy) and endpoint D(Dx, Dy) as $d = \sqrt{\{(S_x \sim D_x)^2 + (S_y \sim D_y)^2\}}$, go to step 10.

Step 7: Identify the region with which the direct path from starting point to the endpoint is constrained.

7.1 Apply the technique with respect to the constrained region, which yields two obstacle-free paths with respect to the current obstacle.

7.2 Check if any of the above two paths are constrained by other obstacles. If so, go to Step 7.4, else go to Step 7.3

7.3 Calculate the path lengths and store the path point's coordinates and length of each path in the results file. Go to step 7.9

7.4 Check if the path is constrained with a single obstacle or two obstacles

7.5 Apply the technique accordingly and obtain obstacle-free subpaths

7.6 Join these subpaths with the main path

7.7 Calculate the lengths of the paths and store the path points and length of each path in the results file

7.8 Check if the second main path is also constrained by other obstacles. If so, repeat the steps 7.4 to 7.7; else go to Step 7.9

7.9 Read the paths data from the results file and arrange the paths in the increasing value of the path lengths

7.10 The first path in the revised results file now gives the shortest obstacle-free path between the starting point and the endpoint. The other paths in the file provide alternate feasible obstacle-free paths with lengths in increasing order, which are more than the optimum value. Go to step 10.

Step 8: Number the two constrained regions with respect to their distance from the starting point. The nearest one is the first region, and the farthest one is the second region. Go to 8.1

8.1 Apply the technique with respect to the two constrained regions.

8.2 Check if any of the above paths are constrained with the third region. If so, go to Step 8.4, else go to Step 8.3

8.3 Calculate the path lengths and store the path points, coordinates and length of each path in the results file. Go to Step 8.8

8.4 Apply the technique and obtain obstacle-free subpaths

8.5 Join these subpaths with the main path

8.6 Calculate the path lengths and store the path points and length of each path in the results file.

8.7 Check if any of the remaining paths is also constrained with the third region. If so, repeat Steps 8.4 to 8.6; else go to step 8.8

8.8 Read the paths data from the results file and arrange the paths in the increasing value of the path lengths.

8.9 The first path in the revised results file now gives the shortest obstacle-free path between the starting point and the endpoint. The other paths in the file provide alternate feasible obstacle-free paths with lengths in increasing order, which are more than the optimum value. Go to step 10

Step 9: Number the three constrained regions with respect to their distance from the starting point. The nearest one will be the first region, the farthest one will be the third region, and the remaining one will be the second region. Go to 9.1

9.1 Apply the technique with respect to the three constrained regions.

9.2 Calculate the path lengths and store the path points, coordinates and length of each path in the results file.

9.3 Read the paths data from the results file and arrange the paths in the increasing value of the path lengths.

9.4 The first path in the revised results file now gives the shortest obstacle-free path between the starting point and the endpoint. The other paths in the file provide alternate feasible obstacle-free paths with lengths in increasing order, which are more than the optimum value.

Step 10: Stop

The following section presents a detailed algorithm along with a flowchart (Figures 3.9 and 3.10) for any number of elliptical objects.

3.1.2.1.4 CCT Algorithm for Any Number of Elliptical Obstacles

Step 1: Start

Step 2: Read the number of ellipses, n.

Step 3: For i = 1; I < = n, repeat: Step 4

Step 4: Input the coordinates of the centre of the ellipse regions and their major and minor axes, angle of orientations; Ci, MJi, MNi, Ai

Step 5: Input the starting point coordinates S (Sx, Sy).

Step 6: Read the endpoint coordinates D (Dx, Dy).

Step 7: Check the type of constraint:

If not constrained with any region, then go to step 8

else go to step 9

Step 8: Find the un-constrained direct Euclidean path distance between the starting point S (Sx, Sy) and the endpoint D (Dx, Dy) as: $d = \sqrt{\{(S_x \sim D_x)^2 + (S_y \sim D_y)^2\}}$

Go to step 9

Step 9: Identify the region with which the direct path from starting point to the endpoint is constrained. Consider ellipses i and i+1. Repeat Step 9 until i = n.

9.1 Apply the technique with respect to the constrained region, which yields two obstacle-free paths with respect to the current obstacle.

9.2 Check if any of the above two paths are constrained by other obstacles. If so, go to Step 9.4; else go to Step 9.3

9.3 Calculate the path lengths and store the path point's coordinates and length of each path in the results file. Go to step 9.9

9.4 Apply the technique and obtain obstacle-free subpaths

9.5 Join these subpaths with the main path

9.6 Calculate the lengths of the paths and store the path points and length of each path in the results file

9.7 Check if the second main path is also constrained by the second obstacle. If so, repeat the steps 9.4 to 9.6; else go to Step 9.9

9.8 Read the paths data from the results file and arrange the paths in the increasing value of the path lengths

9.9 The first path in the revised results file now gives the shortest obstacle-free path between the starting point and the endpoint. The other paths in the file provide alternate feasible obstacle-free paths with lengths in increasing order, which are more than the optimum value. Go to Step 10.

9.10 Increment i++

Step 10: Stop.

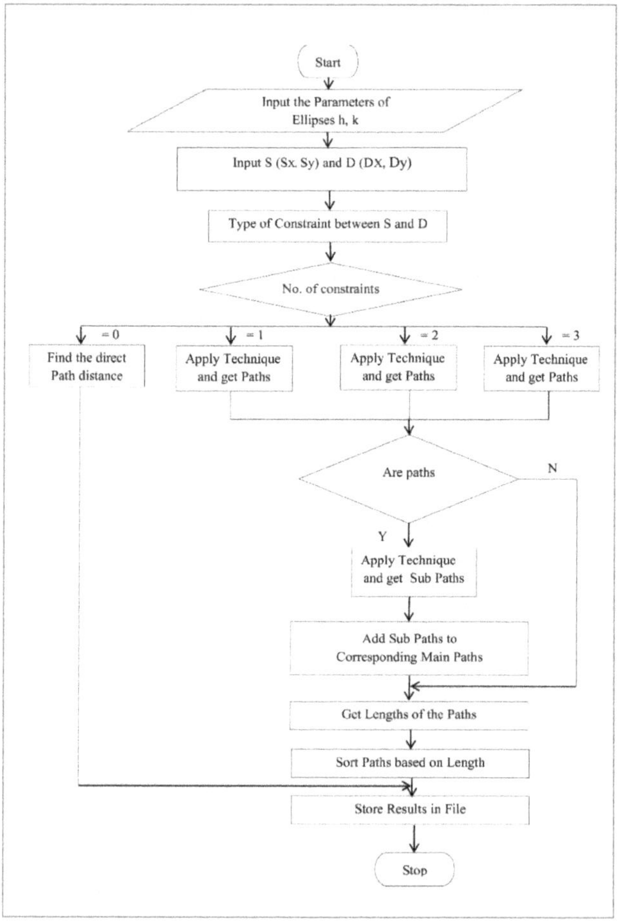

Figure 3.8: CCT Flowchart for Three Elliptical Obstacles

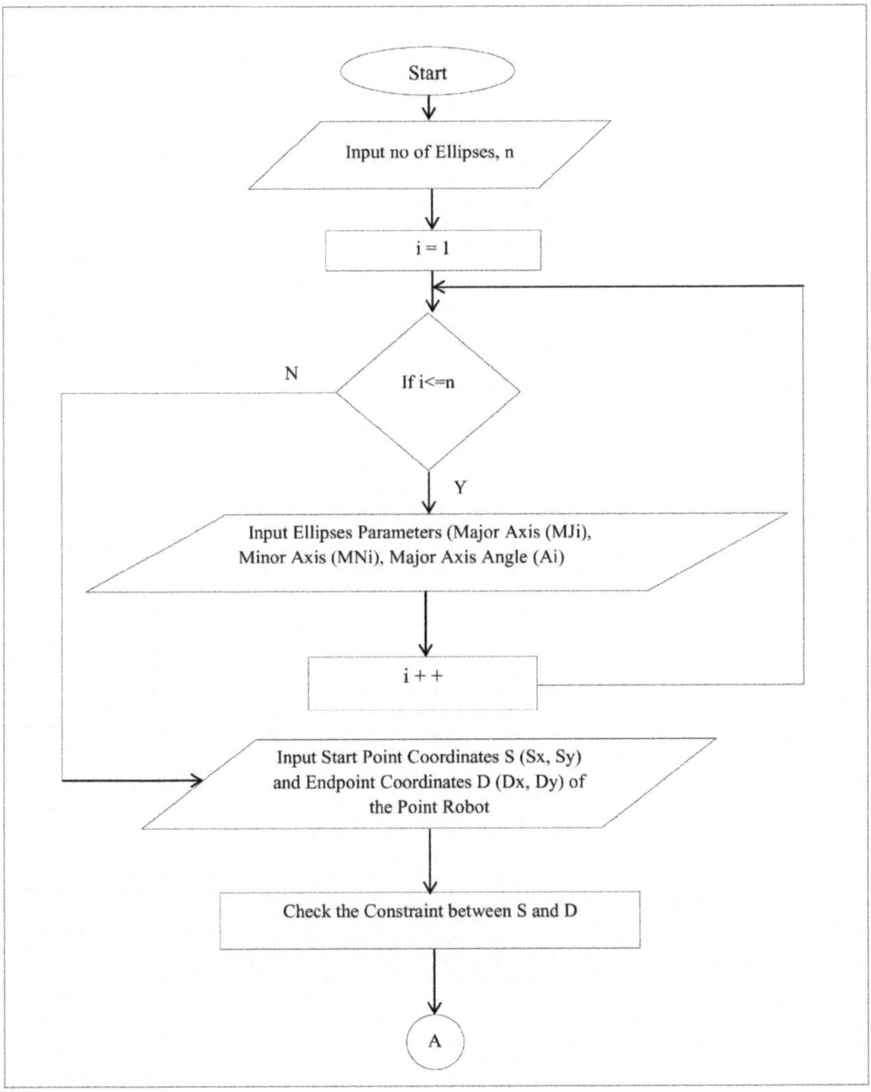

Figure 3.9: CCT Flowchart for Any Number of Elliptical Obstacles (Part A)

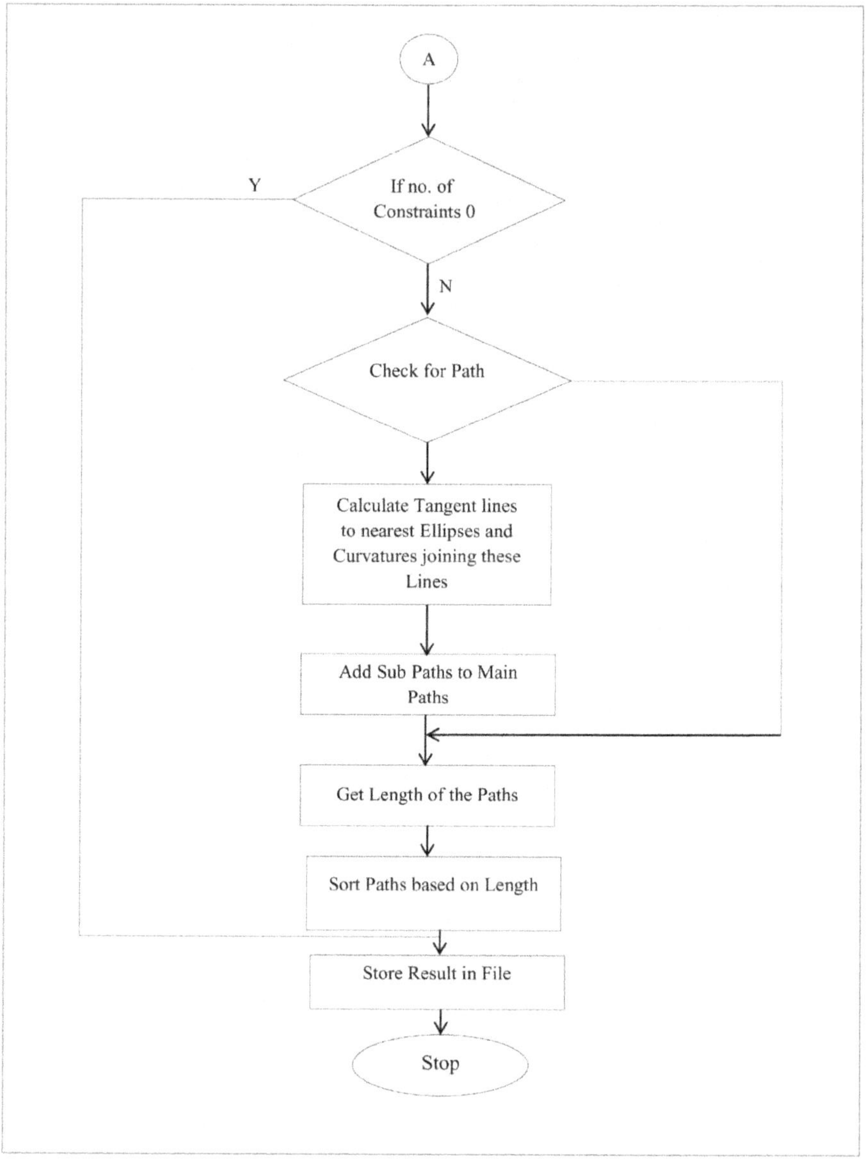

Figure 3.10: CCT Flowchart for Any Number of Elliptical Obstacles (Part B)

3.1.2.2 CRF Protocol

Coordinate Reference Frame (CRF) technique [37] is based upon the definition of a new coordinate frame of reference, find new coordinates for polygonal vertex points using geometrical transformations, and manipulate them to find the unhindered way for a mobile robot. First, using an unconstrained line between the starting point and the endpoint of the robot path as the y-axis, a new coordinate reference frame is defined. The new coordinates of all the vertices of the polygon relative to that coordinate frame are found. Then the vertices are split into two groups according to +x or –x values of their new coordinates and sorted on y values. In order to find the right path, the starting point is joined with each vertex on the right side, i.e., +x side, and the vertex without points on the right side gives the point of the undisturbed solution path. Next, the starting point is moved to this point of resolution, and the above process is repeated until the endpoint is reached. The entire distance from the right path is calculated. The exact process is repeated to obtain the left way solution and the left way distance. The optimal path from the two paths above is determined according to the minimum distance of the path.

3.1.2.3 MPD Protocol

In this section MPD protocol proposed by Ravindranadh [37] is programmed using Matlab® for calculating robot paths moving through a time-varying environment using position information of the first robot and reachable cone of the second robot to determine possible collisions at a future time and thus in a position to avoid them by deviating from the nominal path. Here, one robot is assumed a dynamic obstacle and the other robot's collision-free path is found. In this method, the position of the reachable cone of the robot is mapped in a configuration time-space graph at discrete time intervals taking time in the z-direction. The possible collision with the obstacle is found by checking the intersection of the position circle of the obstacle (C_2) with the base circle (C_1) of the reachable cone of the mobile robot at that discrete time interval.

If $C_1 \cap C_2 = \emptyset$, there is no possible collision, and the robot path is free.

If $C_1 \cap C_2 \neq \emptyset$, then there is a possible collision and path deviation algorithm is to be implemented.

3.1.2.4 SLICE Protocol

Survey, substantiation and plotting of three-dimensional underwater conditions are the biggest challenges in path planning. As per a 2018 report of the National Oceanic and Atmospheric Administration (NOAA), 80% of the underwater environment is unexplored. An underwater environment can be a natural underwater cave, a plant, a submerged manmade object that makes the exploration fascinating, complex and dangerous. The band limit available for underwater communication is minimal and re-echoing, leading to issues of reliability. High-frequency communication in shallow water is a highly challenging task because both underwater and in seabed environments like sea surface waves and ocean medium distorts signal properties.

Three-dimensional environment path planning exhibits a great likelihood, but unlike two-dimensional environment, the complexity gets bigger exponentially with springy constraints. Even though path planning is time-consuming and tedious in such complex three-dimensional environments but once achieved will lay a path for a fascinating underwater exploration. The flow chart for the SLICE protocol is shown in Figure 3.11.

For an in-depth understanding of how the SLICE and 2D3DPP protocol works, the three-dimensional space underwater is defined as follows:

1. The underwater 3D space is defined as $\boldsymbol{\varnothing}$.
2. Depth of the underwater space $\boldsymbol{d_n}$ where n is defined as layer number $\forall$ n $\in$ {0, ∞}.
3. A two-dimensional plane (layer) underwater is defined by $\boldsymbol{L_n}$, where n is defined as layer number $\forall$ n $\in$ {0, ∞}.
4. A submerged (partially or totally) or suspended obstacle defined by $\boldsymbol{O}$
5. The two-dimensional shape formed as a result of the two-dimensional layer ($\boldsymbol{L_n}$) intersecting the 3D obstacle ($\boldsymbol{O}$) is defined by $\boldsymbol{S_n}$, where n is defined as layer number $\forall$ n $\in$ {0, ∞}.
6. $\boldsymbol{L_P}$ is the layer at which the two-dimensional path planning takes place, and $\boldsymbol{d_p}$ is the depth of this layer measured from the surface of the water.

Consideration and Assumptions that have been made in order to execute the "CCT and CRF" combined method. They are listed below,

1. The three-dimensional underwater space is scanned and mapped so as to determine the following aspects,
   a. Depth
   b. Viscosity
   c. Temperature
   d. Current
2. The three-dimensional space is scanned and mapped for obstacles to determine the following aspects
   a. Shape
   b. Size
   c. Number
   d. Position
   e. Static or dynamic
3. The three-dimensional underwater space is assumed to be void to any current, temperature changes and dynamic obstacles.

3.1.2.4.1 SLICE Algorithm

Step 1: Start

Step 2: Input Starting point (S) and Endpoint (D) includes depth of starting point d_S and depth of endpoint d_T

Step 3: Input all layers data L_n

Step 4: Determine shapes of obstacle S_O

Step 5: Determine the number of obstacles N

Step 6: Determine Layer Set L_A

Step 7: Determine Depth Set d_A

Step 8: Determine Layer with Largest Area L_O

Step 9: Execute single-axis path @ $d_S \sim d_O$

Step 10: Call CCT or CRF or Hybrid

Step 11: Stop

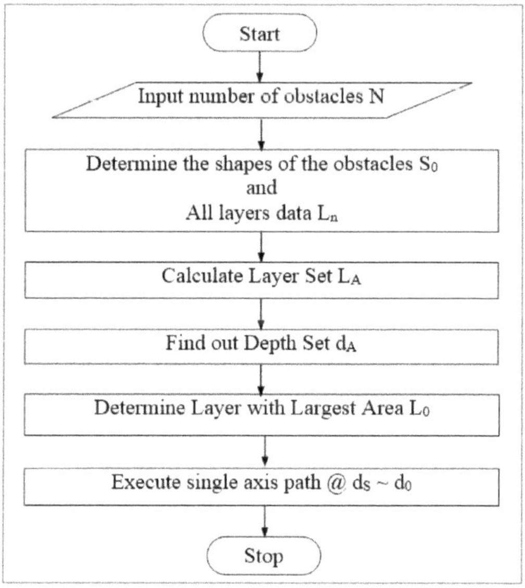

Figure 3.11: Flowchart for SLICE Protocol

3.1.2.5 2D3DPP Protocol

The protocol under disclosure proposes a novel method to traverse either a two-dimensional space or a three-dimensional space in a shorter period and in a more application-specific (planar or underwater) manner. This protocol is for a single robot with static obstacles. For two-dimensional, obstacles can be ellipses, polygons or a combination of both. For three-dimensional, obstacles can be of any regular shape like a cylinder, cone, prism, pyramid, and sphere or can be of any irregular shape.

The technique under consideration also offers to address all of the disadvantages of three-dimensional path planning underwater, such as time delays, a lack of computational connection, and restrictive/unnecessary parallel processing in a mainly static environment.

The disclosed protocol overcomes the limitations of underwater computational hardware by implementing the SLICE protocol, which not only requires less processing power but also has the ability to reduce computation time by perceiving the three-dimensional underwater space as a stack of infinite two-dimensional layers of unit thickness.

Furthermore, this technique aims to divide the three-dimensional path planning procedures into co-dependent two-dimensional path planning and a single axis depth traversing. For two-dimensional route planning, the CCT, CRF, and HYBRID protocols are utilised.

In general, any underwater systems utilize a propeller mechanism paired with a controlled water inlet chamber which allows the system to realize any coordinates in the three-dimensional space. This method although, very practical for path planning, object tracking and dynamic obstacle avoidance in three-dimensional spaces above or below the ground, has limitations such as high computational requirements.

Since a majority of the obstacles encountered underwater tend to be static, this level of computational complexity adds to a time delay and hardware requirement in spaces that are generally submerged in water.

These limitations have been successfully addressed by the protocol under disclosure, the "2D3DPP protocol", for which Figure 3.12 is the flowchart. All the mathematical protocols developed are programmed in Matlab® software for computations.

3.1.2.5.1 2D3DPP Algorithm

Step 1: Start

Step 2: Input starting point (S) and endpoint (T) includes depth of starting point d_S and depth of endpoint DT

Step 2: Input all layers data L_n

Step 3: Determine shapes of obstacle S_O

Step 4: Determine the number of obstacles N

Step 5: Determine Layer Set L_A

Step 6: Determine Depth Set d_A

Step 7: Determine Layer with Largest Area L_O

Step 10: Execute single-axis path @ $d_S \sim d_O$

Step 8: If So is all curved, call "CCT" with S ($d_S \sim d_O$), T ($d_T \sim d_O$), N, L_O

Else If So is all polygonal, call "CRF" with S ($d_S \sim d_O$), T ($d_T \sim d_O$), N, L_O

Else, call "Hybrid Technique" with S ($d_S \sim d_O$), T ($d_T \sim d_O$), N, L_O

Step 9: Read path coordinates

Step 11: Execute Path Coordinates from Step 9

Step 11: Execute single-axis oath @ $d_T \sim d_O$

Step 12: Stop

3.2 Experimental Strategies using Reactive Techniques

Because the subject of this research is a comparison of classical and reactive approaches, all experiments are performed using the reactive methodologies. The input data used for Mathematical protocols is normalized and used in experiments.

3.2.1 Approach for Experimentation

A consistent strategy is taken for all experiments. Initially, the robot is animated to aid comprehension; afterwards, a Mechatronics design method is applied to develop the robot, including the control system. Later, the chassis and other mechanical elements that will connect with the embedded system are built. This robot is tested on the chosen arena.

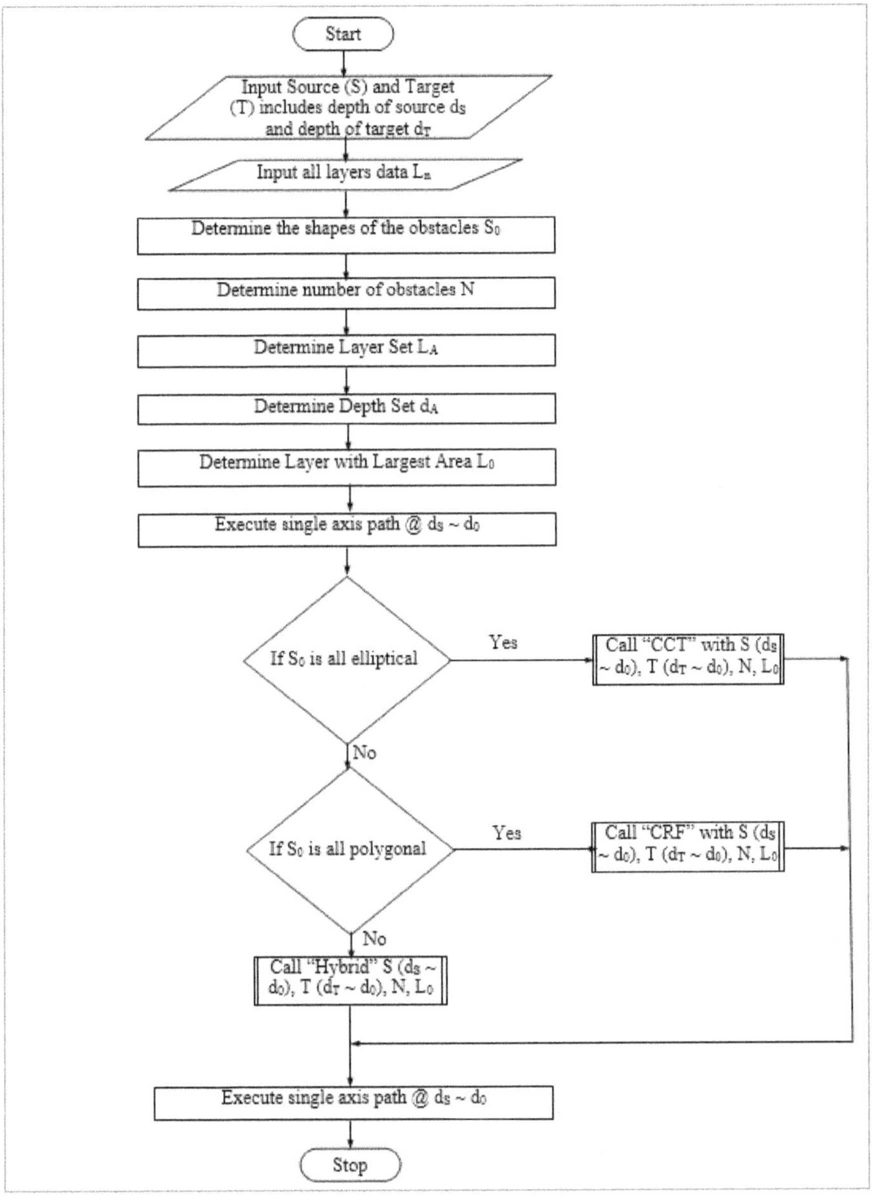

Figure 3.12: 2D3DPP Flowchart

3.2.1.1 Visual Creation

Using 3DS Max®, Adobe Pro®, Adobe Premier Pro®, animation software, the robot, obstacles are created for initial understanding. This robot will be animated along the estimated path avoiding obstacles.

3.2.1.2 Mechatronics Approach for Design and Manufacturing

The Mechatronics approach is the combination of Mechanical Engineering, Electronics Engineering and Software Engineering, broadly stated. While rejecting splitting engineering into various disciplines, it emphasizes their inter-dependency to create a product in the real world.

3.2.1.2.1 Parallel Design

Parallel design is an interdisciplinary modern design process; this involves the simultaneous selection, assessment, integration and optimisation of the system, all subsystems within it, and components as a whole. All design disciplines operate in parallel and in collaboration throughout the design and development process to achieve optimum overall design, as shown in Figure 3.13.

3.2.1.2.2 Electronics

For any machine to work, electrical components are an essential part. With the developments in manufacturing processes, new and developed electronics came into the forefront. Any machine requires a power supply, and in modern days, electronic circuits have become an integral part. Electronic circuits, whether simple resistors and capacitors or sophisticated microcontrollers, have become the core of any modern machine.

3.2.1.2.3 Software

The electronic components form the hardware of the working circuit. When the applications are of this magnitude, the software is an essential component along with the electronics. While the electronic components play the role of being the structure of the circuit, the software integrates the hardware with the electronic actuators. In this experiment, to integrate various electronic modules and to execute various commands, a fair amount of software programming is employed.

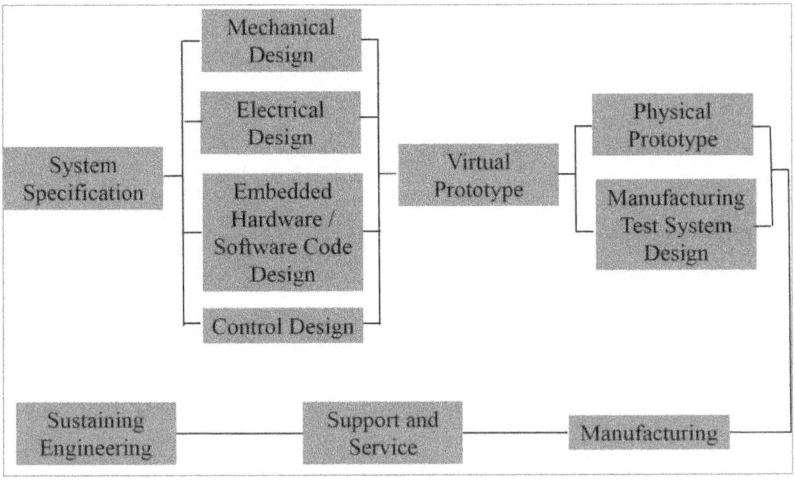

Figure 3.13: Mechatronics Parallel Design

3.2.1.2.4 Mechanical Design

After the electronic and software technologies give outputs, the design of the robot is made. After considering the weight of the circuits and other components, and the end effectors of the robot, the material for the robot and motors are chosen. By building a chassis and a body with the help of mechanical processes like bending, welding, brazing, etc. and mounting the motors onto the chassis, the physical shape of the robot is built.

3.2.2 Experimental setup for Two-dimensional Static Obstacle Avoidance Robot

The primary purpose of this robot is to cross ahead autonomously and to change direction if it meets a significant obstacle on its way. The robot will prevent any obstruction large enough to be detected by the forward-mounted infrared sensor.

There is a distributed load (assumed to be uniform) of 0.8 kg on the chassis by the various components like circuits, batteries, end effectors, self-weight, motors, body and other mountings on it. It is similar to a beam subjected to a uniformly distributed load. Based on the concepts from Beams in Strength of Materials, the dimensions of the chassis are 200 mm x 200 mm x 70 mm are arrived at for a metal sheet material of 1.5

mm thickness. Figures 3.14 to 3.16 shows the chassis, the body, and the final assembly of the robot designed in Creo®.

Figure 3.14: Chassis designed in Creo®

The first step is to build the robot itself, which includes a two-rear wheel drive and a roller wheel on the front. 12 V battery motors power the two rear wheels. The caster is affixed to the front of the robot. This wheel allows the front of the robot to move freely, along with providing stability to the entire robot.

Figure 3.15: Body designed in Creo®

The next stage is to install the hardware needed to feed the robot and operate the wheels. An L298 motor driver powers the wheels. Basing on the popular dual h – bridge motor diver integrated circuit, the L298 motor driver is developed. This module is beneficial in controlling both engines back and forth quickly and independently. A digital rotary encoder connected to one of the wheels calculates the path travelled. A combination of three infrared sensors is the obstacle avoiding capability of the robot to detect any obstacles. Arduino Uno R3 micro-controller is used to process the data sensed by the sensors and thus drive the motors appropriately.

The code is straightforward and can be divided into three sections. Setup function: In this, pins 6, 9, 10 and 11 act as output pins, which have the pulse-width-modulation feature for controlling the robot's speed. The L298 motor-driver input pins are connected to these 6, 9, 10, 11 output pins. In addition, the forward-mounted infrared sensors of the robot are connected to two additional general-purpose input-output pins on the micro-controller, which provide a voltage of 5 V to the sensors.

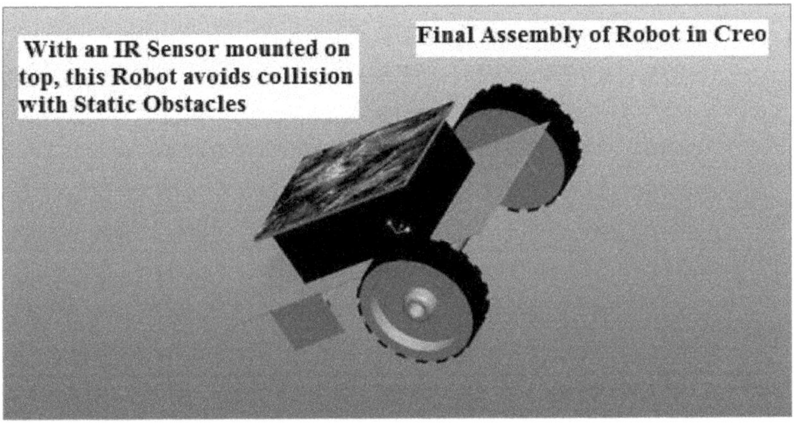

Figure 3.16: Final Assembly designed in Creo®

For the loop function, read the value of the analogue sensor from the infrared sensors; a flag is raised if the robot detects an obstacle. The potentiometer allows the sensor to be set to detect an obstacle at a distance. When a barrier is detected by the infra-red sensors, a flag is raised, and the program enters a specific loop, in which the robot decides whether to turn left or right according to which side the obstacle was detected. If the left infrared sensor detects an obstacle, the robot briefly backs up and rotates to the right; else, if the right infrared sensor detects an obstacle, the robot briefly backs up and rotates to the left. The robot retreats briefly, move away from the obstacle and begins to advance again. By default, the robot continues to progress until another barrier is

detected. `

3.2.2.1 Parts Used

1) Infra-Red Obstacle Avoidance Sensor: A miniaturized IR transmitter and receiver module for infrared remote control system is used for the experiment. This IR sensor has a PIN diode and a preamplifier is assembled on the lead frame. The epoxy package contains an IR hardware filter and works on LED principle. The Infrared Obstacle Avoidance Sensor has a pair of infrared transmitting and receiving sensors. The infrared LED emits Infrared signals and when an obstacle appears on the line of infrared light, it is reflected back by the obstacle which is sensed by the receiver. This sensor is having three pins, one for OUT, one for GND and one for Supply Voltage. TSOP 38238 type sensor obtained from the makers Vishay is used in the experimentation. Dimensions of the IR Sensor: 5.0 mm width x 6.95 mm height x 4.8 mm depth. The weight of the sensor is 5 g. The specifications include a supply voltage in the range of 2.5 to 5.5 V, supply current of 3 mA, operating temperature in the range of -25 to +85 °C and a 10° incidence angle. Rated distance measuring range of the sensor is 15 to 30 cm. The sensitivity of the sensor is 0.12 mW/m^2. The response time of the sensor is 60 ms.

   Sensor Calibration: Because of the physical property of IR sensors, the returned voltage times amps value is inversely proportional to the distance it senses. The integer value read from analog input pin is proportional to the voltage times amps input. As a result, the integer value returned by analog is inversely proportional to the distance measured. An obstacles is put in front of the sensors from 10 cm to 50 cm and the measured integer values are kept for every 5 cm. Then a linear regression is performed for 1/measured integer values and corresponding distance. Especially the values corresponding to the rated distance range of the sensor, i.e., 15 to 30 cm are considered and the corresponding sensitivity is calculated. As the sensor's sensitivity is around all four directions, the area it covers is considered. The value obtained is 0.12 mW/m^2 and is as mentioned in the catalogue.

2) Microcontroller: Arduino Uno R3 – Atmega 328 PP (32 KB flash memory) with 6-20 V input voltage range, 14 digital I/O pins.
3) Motor Driver: L298N motor driver with 46 V maximum operating voltage and 2 A peak output current per channel.
4) Robot Chassis: 200 x 200 x 70 mm with a sheet thickness of 1.5 mm.
5) Motors: 12 V DC Motor with 200 RPM rated speed, 1.5 kg-cm rated torque.
6) One container to hold the battery.
7) Two wheels of 10 cm diameter each.
8) One caster wheel: Swivel caster wheel of 2.1 cm wheel diameter.

3.2.3 Experimental setup for Two-dimensional Dynamic Obstacle Avoidance Robots

This experimentation is done in the lines of Swarm Intelligence. Swarm Intelligence is a novel distributed smart paradigm to solve optimization problems, which was initially based on biological examples by flocking, rearing and swarming events in vertebrates. Swarm intelligence can be for a natural or artificial system. It is a collective behaviour of distribution and self-regulation. The concept is used in studies of AI. Swarm-intelligent systems generally consist of a population of simple agents or organisms that interact locally with each other and with their surroundings. There are very straightforward rules to be followed by the group. Although there is no centralised control structure governing the behaviour of individual agents, local and to a certain degree random globally, these interactions between these agents lead to the development of intelligent global behaviour without the knowledge of individual agents. Swarm intelligence science is multi-disciplinary. It can be studying the science of biological systems in the name of natural swarming or the human remembrances as artificial swarming. To understand the fundamental mechanism, the scientific mainstream is trying to model the swarm systems and to address practical issues in so many application areas; the engineering stream is following the insights developed by the scientific group.

3.2.3.1 Scope of Swarm Principles in the Experimentation

In the present experiment, where the coordinates of the endpoint are transmitted to the master robot, retaining one endpoint location, it transmits another location to the slave robot. The two begin to move toward their endpoint and continue to communicate with one another. In the event of a collision, the master robot will continue to its location on its original path, whereas the other robot, the slave, will deviate from its path to avoid the collision. Thus, a cooperative system of individual robots interacting with one another and doing tasks is created. On a more significant level, if more of these robots are considered to perform tasks in this way, it is called imitating the behaviour of the swarm.

However, since the robots do not co-operate to sweep over any area, solve problems to find optimum solutions or have any learning mechanism and do not employ any swarm algorithms as mentioned above, it would be inappropriate to call this particular experiment a direct application of Swarm intelligence.

Hence, in this experiment, only the Swarm behaviour was studied and was adapted. The way the robots behave and perform the given tasks is an inspiration drawn from observation of Swarm behaviour in social insects.

3.2.3.2 GSM – Zigbee Combination

A GSM module is used to read the two endpoint coordinates sent from a mobile phone to one of the robots (arbitrarily called the Master). The Master, retaining one location, passes on the other endpoint location to the other robot (arbitrarily called the Slave) using the Zigbee wireless communication system. Knowing their own present locations by virtue of their onboard GPS systems and having the endpoint locations, the robots compare the two and traverse towards the endpoint location. They keep on communicating using the Zigbee wireless communication system.

3.2.3.3 Design Parameters

The Design includes chassis; body, end effector, locomotion, etc. are detailed below:

Chassis is designed for an estimated distributed load of 3 kg (assumed to be uniform) by the various components like circuits, batteries, end effectors, self-weight, motors, body and other mountings on it. The dimensions of the chassis are 420 mm x 240 mm x 70 mm are arrived at for an acrylic material of 4 mm thickness.

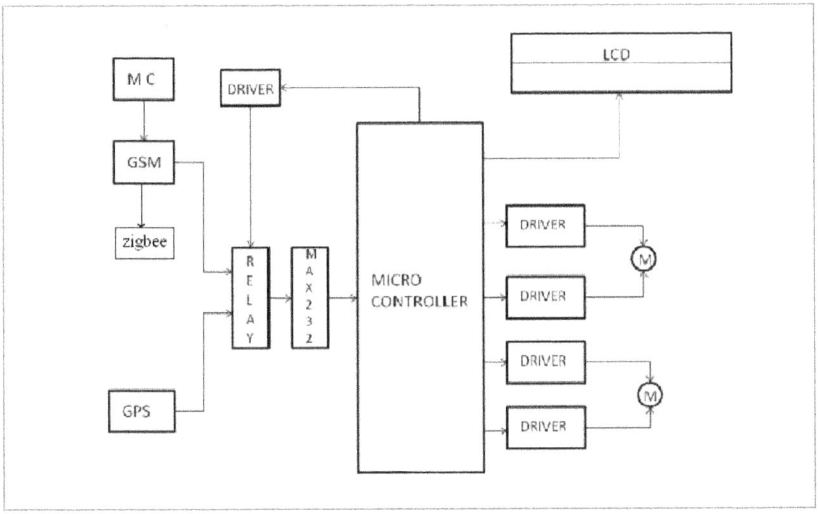

Figure 3.17: Block diagram of the Master Robot Controller

The track used is as shown in Figure 3.27, in which the distance between any two big wheels is 80 mm. The big wheels are known as the suspension wheels, while the smaller wheels are the drive wheels.

a. This is one of the better tracks available for the design since it includes suspension wheels that can take a lot of weight and other vibration effects that help the robot stay stable.

b. Track is also efficient in climbing the uphill roads and other various terrains.

c. The varied dynamic loads on the robot are quickly balanced by these tracks.

d. The wheels align with the track if there is any disturbance in track position this self-aligning track.

e. Dimensions of the suspension wheel are 60 mm in diameter, while the drive wheel is 40 mm.

Figures 3.17 and 3.18 shows the circuit diagrams of the master robot and slave robot, respectively. The first robot has GPS, GSM, and Zigbee, with GPS being used to determine the robot's current coordinates from a satellite. GSM is for sending the endpoint coordinates directly to the master robot and indirectly to the slave robot. Zigbee is for sending the endpoint coordinates to the slave robot through GSM. Other than these components, the micro-controller is for controlling the robots navigation according to the present and endpoint coordinates. Drivers are for controlling motor rotation for navigation and for switching the serial communication from GSM to GPS and vice versa. MAX232 is for converting TTL logic levels to CMOS and vice versa. GPS, GSM, Zigbee are in TTL logic, whereas the microcontroller used in this experiment is CMOS logic. So in order to make communication possible, MAX232 is used as an interface. In the slave robot, Zigbee is used to receive the coordinates from the master robot and for the communication between the two robots. Similarly, the slave robot contains a GPS to know the present coordinates and the endpoint. There is no GSM in the slave robot as the master controls it.

Both the robots will have associative circuitry, as shown in the circuit diagram (Figure 3.19). The circuitry is the basic working system in the robots, which takes feedback from all the components and controls the motors accordingly through relays. The relays are programmed in such a manner that when both the relays are simultaneously on or off, it makes the robot stop. Similarly, the present coordinates of the robot and the endpoint coordinates are displayed in the LCD display. The display is interfaced to port 3 in the micro-controller at pin 10. The GPS continually follows the satellite signal and transmits it to the microcontroller, which calculates the travelled path. Similarly, the coordinates from the user reach the GSM on the master robot 1 through pin 11. The micro-controller in the master robot takes the first coordinate and sends it to the slave robot through Zigbee. The Zigbee on the slave robot receives the signal and sends it to the micro-controller embedded in it. Thus, both the robots will get the coordinates and start tracking individually with establishing communication through Zigbee. The Zigbee on the master robot continuously sends test signals to maintain a communication link with the slave.

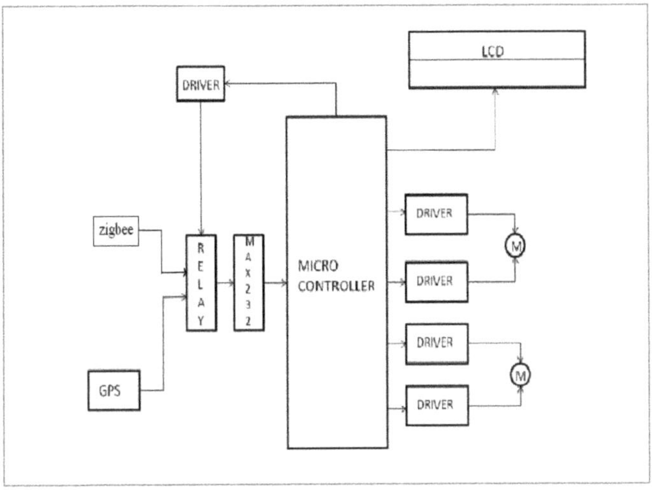

Figure 3.18: Block diagram of the Slave Robot Controller

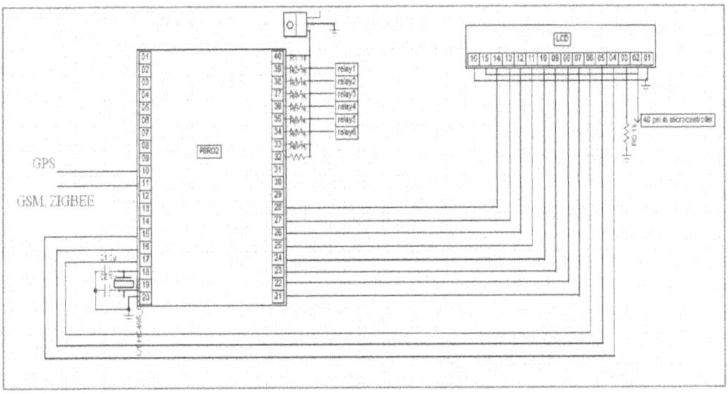

Figure 3.19: Circuit diagram of the microcontroller

The experiment explains the interface between the P89V51RD2BN micro-controller and the Global System for Mobile communication module and the "Hyper Terminal". Hyper Terminal is a Windows application. Hyper Terminal sends the "AT" commands to the Global System for Mobile communication module. The response and the result codes are received in the micro-controller and relayed to the Hyper Terminal. Figures 3.20 and 3.21 show the interfacing of the GSM with the controller.

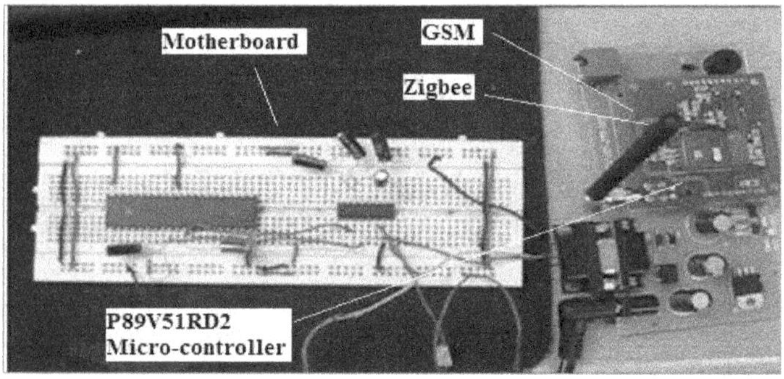

Figure 3.20: Interfacing GSM with controller

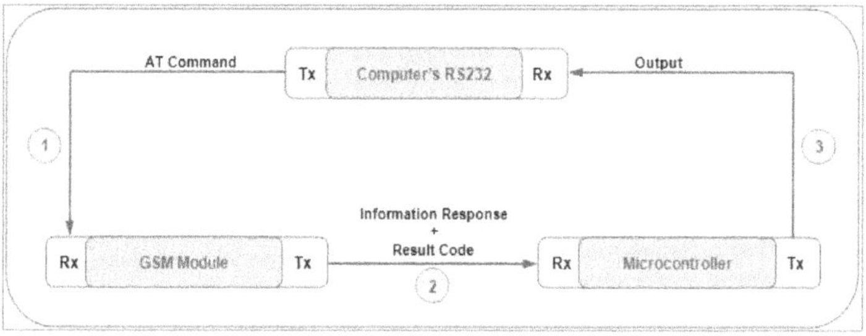

Figure 3.21: GSM interfacing

An RS232 interface for serial communication with an external device is attached to the global system for mobile communication. The transmit-pin (Tx) of the computer's serial port is connected with the receive-pin (Rx) of the global system for the mobile communication module's RS – 232, the transmit-pin (Tx) of the RS - 232 of the global system for the mobile communication module is connected to receive-pin (Rx) of microcontroller's serial transmission-pin, and the micro-controller serial transmission-pin is connected to the receiver pin of the computer serial port.

The microcontroller is programmed to receive and transmit data with a capacity of 9600 bauds. The controller can receive data signals through either random sampling or using the serial interrupt. During the query, the controller continuously scans the serial port for the input data of the Global System for Mobile communication module. In this experimentation, the interruption was used to monitor and control the data flow by the controller in place of the sampling method.

3.2.3.4 Animated Design using Autodesk 3Ds Max®

As shown in the Figures 3.22 and 3.23, the robots, their communication, their work is animated using 3Ds Max®.

3.2.3.5 Robot Design

The experiment was initially started with the design in the CATIA® (Figures 3.24 to 3.26, 3.28, and 3.29) so that the initial allocation of the weight and other features are well assembled for the functioning of the robots and the aesthetic look. The circuit is designed in which the micro controller is embedded with other technologies like GPS, GSM and Zigbee and the motors drivers.

The chassis is formed next in the process by heating the acrylic material and then bending it into the desired shape. The chassis houses the motors, wheels, and tracks. The body is designed for the protection of the various parts of the robots, so it is made of acrylic material, and it is heated and bent into the required shape. Then it is attached to the chassis using L clamps. Figures 3.30 to 3.34 and 3.36 shows the fabrication and assembly of the components. The next step is to install the circuits on the board. The two robots are programmed using the Keil® software (Figure 3.35).

Figure 3.22: Snapshot of Computer Animation

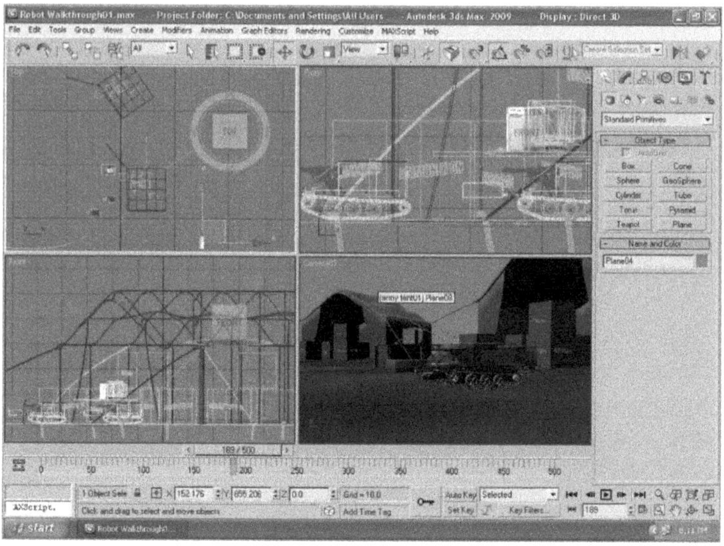

Figure 3.23: Snapshot of 3DS MAX

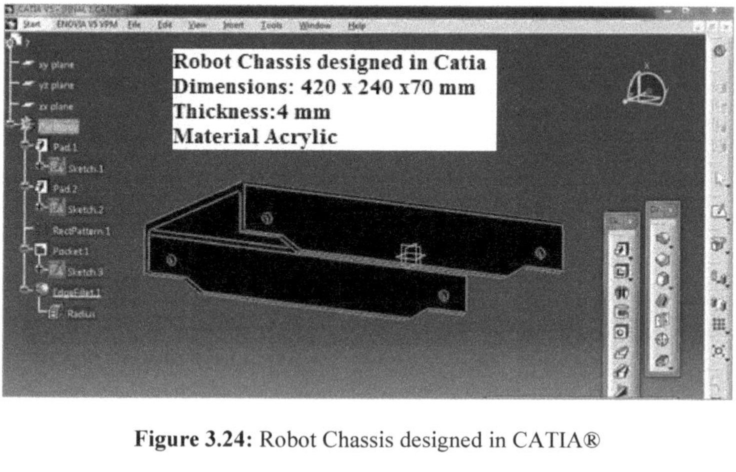

Figure 3.24: Robot Chassis designed in CATIA®

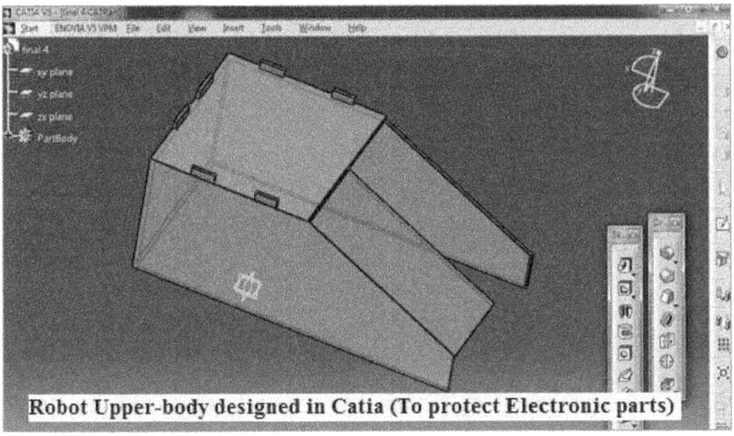

Figure 3.25: Robot Upper body designed in CATIA®

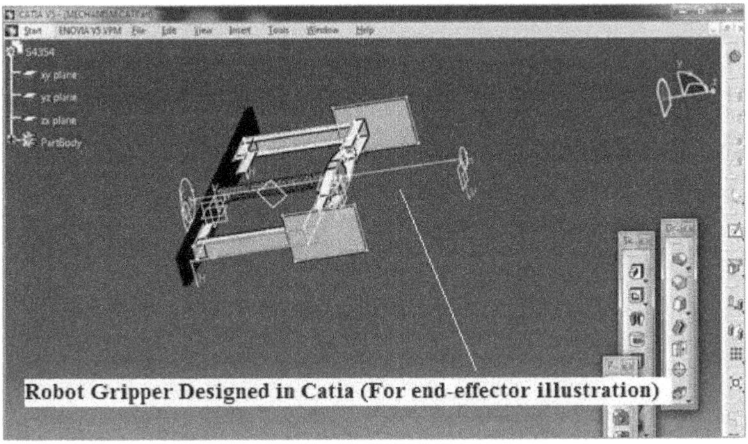

Figure 3.26: Robot Gripper/Picker designed in CATIA® (End effector – For demonstration)

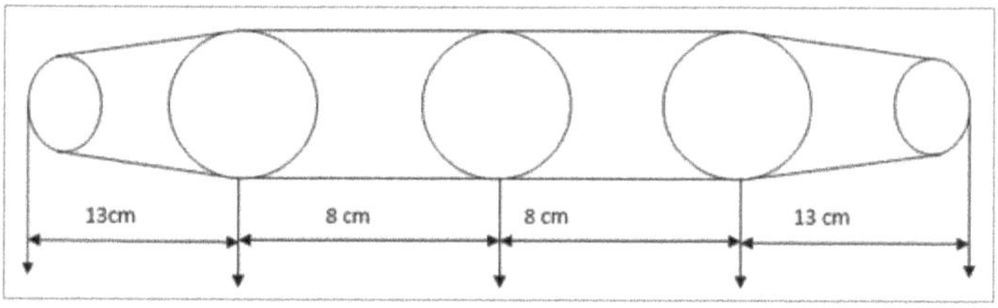

Figure 3.27: Robot Belt Drive

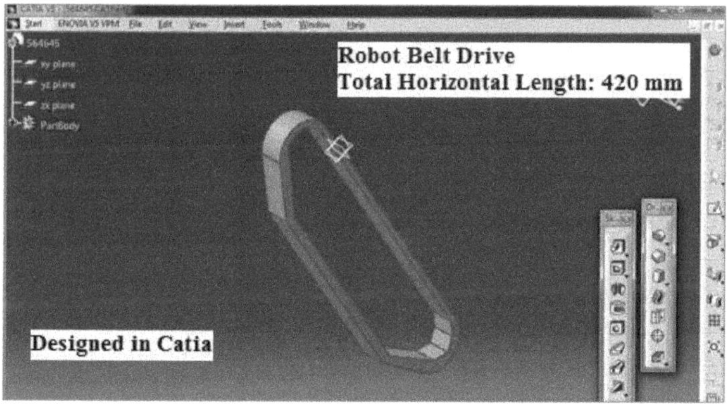

Figure 3.28: Robot Belt Drive designed in CATIA®

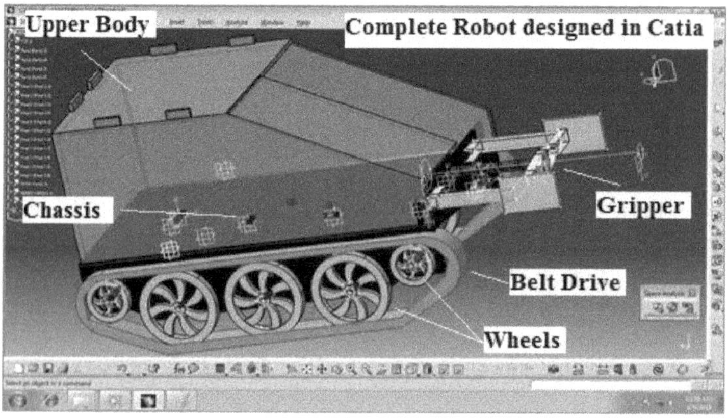

Figure 3.29: Total Robot designed in CATIA®

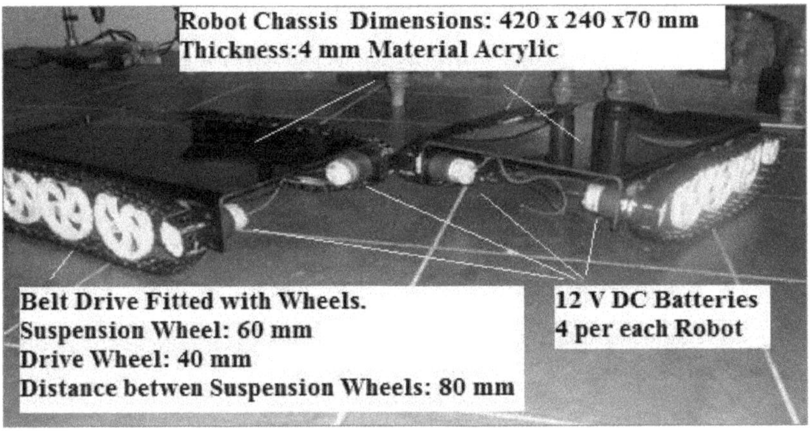

Figure 3.30: Fabricated Chassis

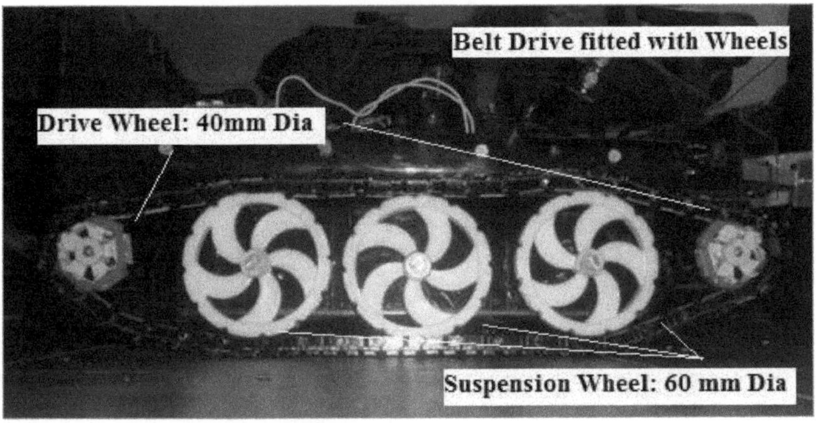

Figure 3.31: Robot Track

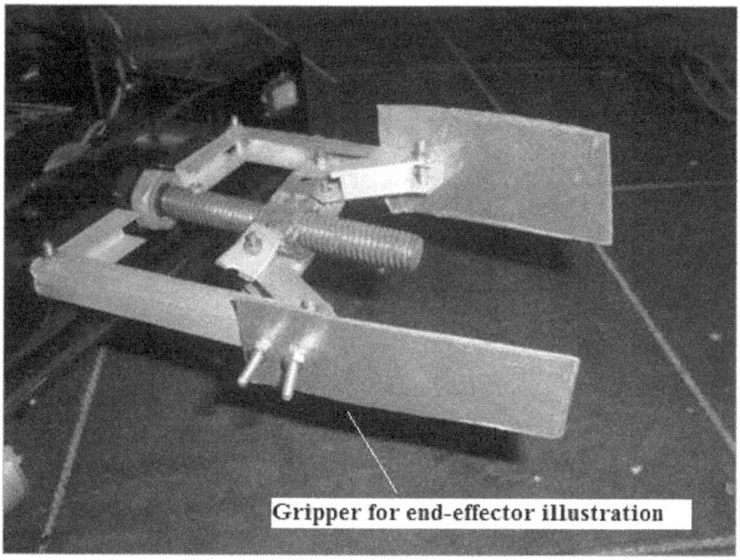

Figure 3.32: Gripper (End effector – For demonstration)

Figure 3.33: Robot

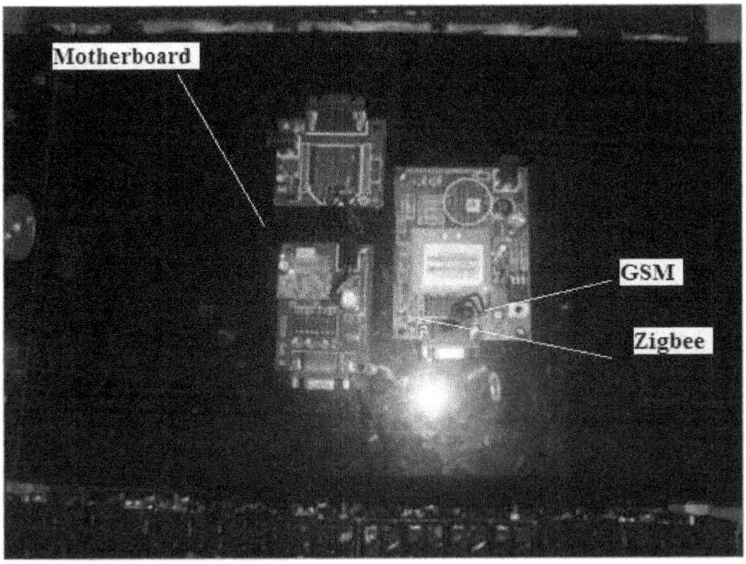

Figure 3.34: Motherboard

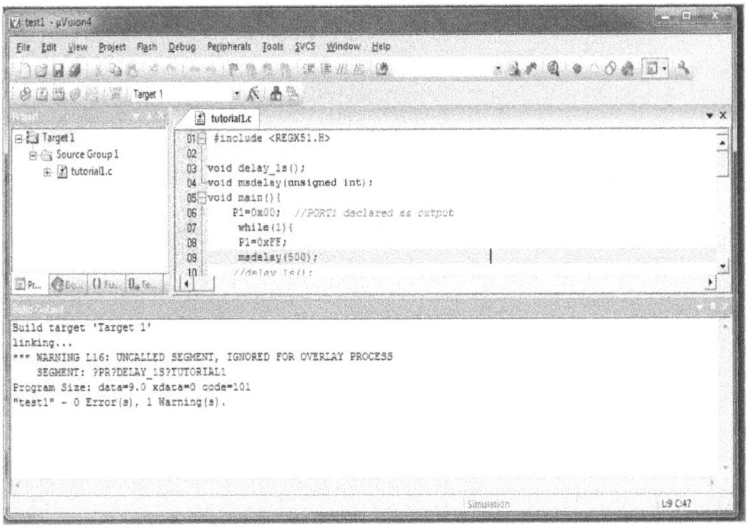

Figure 3.35: Source Code

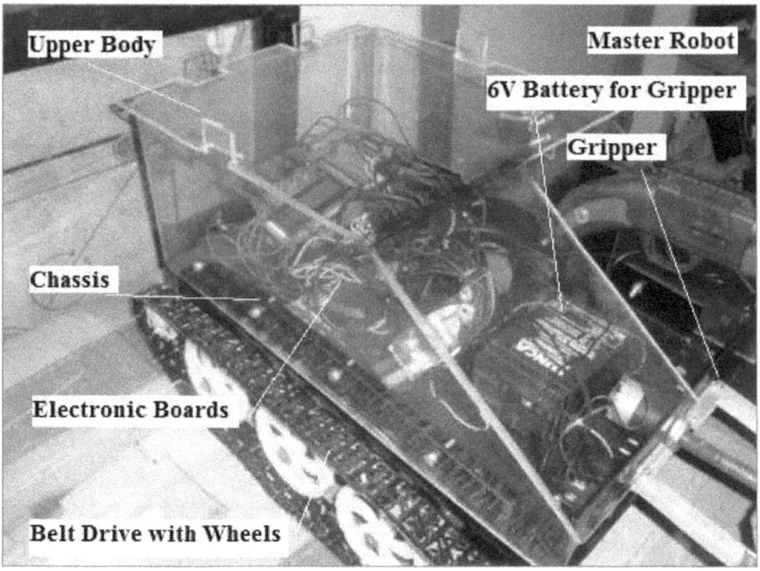

Figure 3.36: Final Master Robot

3.2.3.6 AT Commands

The AT controls are instructions for controlling the modem. AT stands for ATtention. Each command line begins with 'AT' or 'at'. This is the reason why modem commands are termed AT commands.

3.2.3.7 Zigbee

Zigbee will have an onboard regulator of 3.3 V with a maximum limit of 250 mA and a level switchover circuit to connect to 5 V circuits. Two light-emitting diodes are used for associate power and activity. 2 mm sockets with 10-pin each are included to protect the modem. This also allows convenient recycling, upgrading and swapping. All commonly used pins are output along the edge, making it convenient to breadboard or thread up. They are specially designed to be used with a Future Technology Devices International (FTDI) cable to connect to a PC via USB. This means setting up or upgrading the adaptor painlessly just by connecting a cable.

3.2.3.8 Micro-controller

The P89V51RD2 micro-controller belongs to the 80C51 microcontroller family series. This microcontroller is equipped with 1024 bytes of data RAM and a 64 kB Flash. One key functionality of the P89V51RD2 is its X2 mode option. This can be executed with either the conventional 80C51 clock rate of 12 clocks/machine or the X2 mode of 6 clocks/machine to achieve twice the output at the same clock frequency.

3.2.3.9 Algorithm for Master Robot

1) GPS ON /* The GPS for master robot is ON */

2) GPS READ /* Read the present locations of Master Robot from the GPS */

3) ARRAY FILL a1 /* Collect the present location coordinates from the GPS and store them in an array a1 */

4) GSM ON /* The GSM is ON */

5) GSM SEND /* Send both the endpoint locations coordinates via message*/

6) GSM READ /* The first endpoint location coordinates are read */

ZIGBEE SEND /* The second endpoint coordinate locations are sent from the Master robot to the Slave robot through Zigbee */

7) ARRAY FILL a2 /* Collect the endpoint location coordinates from the GPS and it in an array a2 */

8) COMPARE a1 & a2/* Comparing the present and endpoint locations */

9) MOTOR CONTROLS/* Left, Right, Front, Back operations performed by the motors based on the comparison of the locations */

10) END /* End of the program */

3.2.3.10 Algorithm for Slave Robot

1) GPS ON /* The GPS for Slave Robot is ON */

2) GPS READ/* Read the present location of Slave Robot from the GPS */

3) ARRAY FILL a3 /* Collect the present location coordinates of the Slave Robot from the GPS and store it in an array a3 */

4) GSM ON /* The GSM is ON */

5) GSM SEND /* Send both the endpoint location coordinates via message*/

ZIGBEE READ /* Read the endpoint coordinates from the Master Robot to the Slave Robot through Zigbee */

6) ARRAY FILL a4 /* Collect the second endpoint location coordinates from the Zigbee and it in an array a4 */

7) COMPARE a3 & a4 /* Comparing the present and endpoint locations */

8) MOTOR CONTROLS /* Left, Right, Front, Back operations performed by the motors based on the comparison of the locations*/

9) END /* End of the program */

3.2.4 Experimental setup for Three-dimensional Static Obstacle Avoidance Robot

By considering the pros and cons of all the materials, PVC pipe has been selected in which all the circuits and wires will be inserted, and the end caps are used to close the ends with motors mounted. Hindustan brand pipe with 63 mm outer diameter, which can withstand a maximum 78.45 N/cm^2 working pressure, is selected.

Four 12 V DC motors have been selected to attain the motion of the vehicle. They have as high as 1200 rpm, which helps to attain the correct movement underwater. Each motor has a 2.3 mm diameter shaft, 2 pins connector, cylindrical magnetic gear, and these motors are generally used for the electronic game machine, electronic toys, car toys, robots, electronic equipment, etc. Paraffin wax is used to seal the motors. Three-blade propellers are used in the experimentation. 250 g of dead weight is added at the bottom of the robot to attain balance. The motor driver, seen in Figure 3.40, is a MOSFET H-bridge that controls all four motors. Figures 3.37 to 3.39 shows the schematic diagrams of the AUV. Figures 3.41 to 3.42 shows the material used to fabricate, and Figure 3.43 completely assembled AUV.

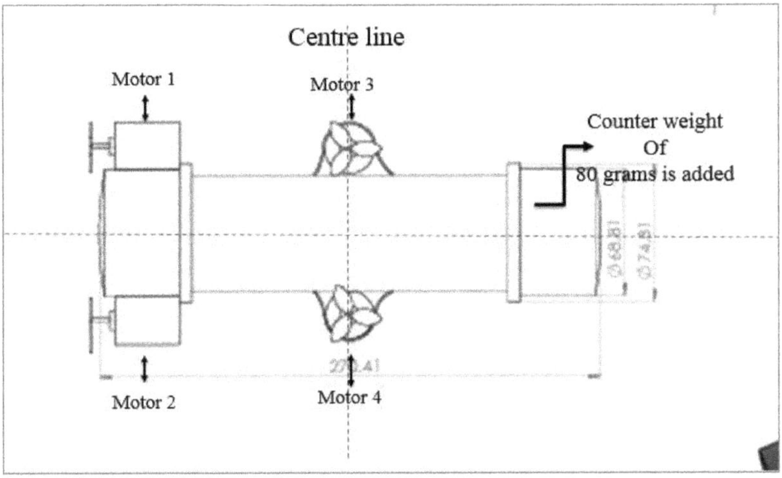

Figure 3.37: Top View of the Autonomous Underwater Vehicle

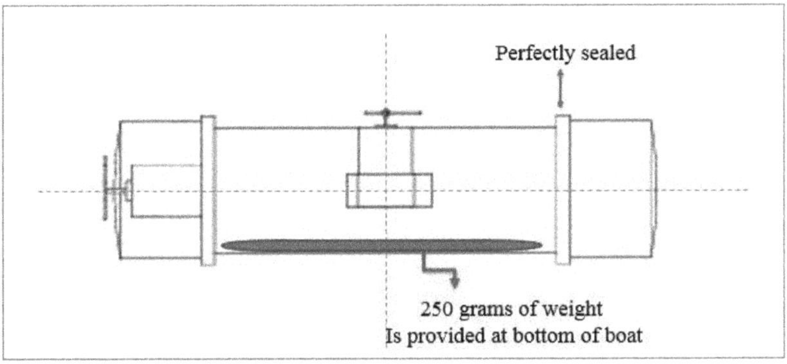

Figure 3.38: Front View of the Autonomous Underwater Vehicle

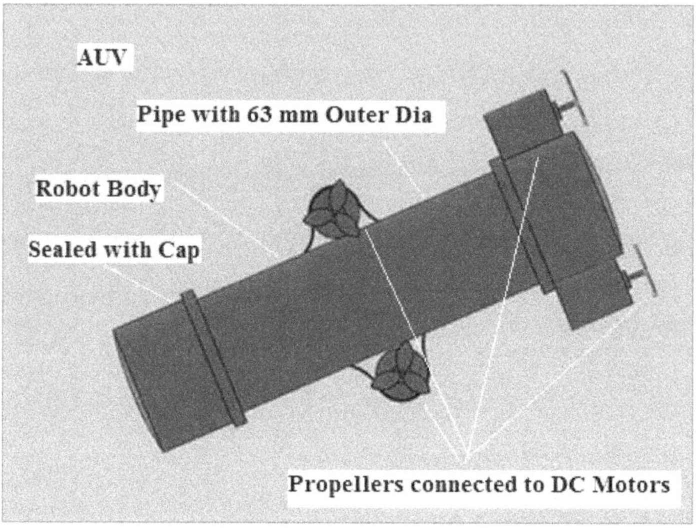

Figure 3.39: Autonomous Underwater Vehicle designed in Creo®

Figure 3.40: MOSFET

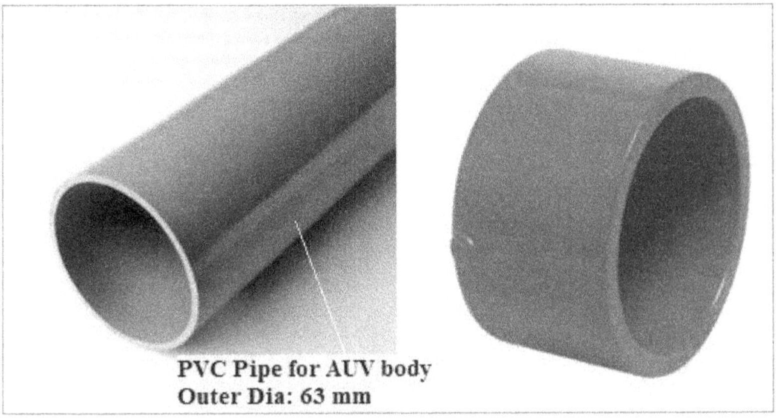

Figure 3.41: PVC pipe for AUV

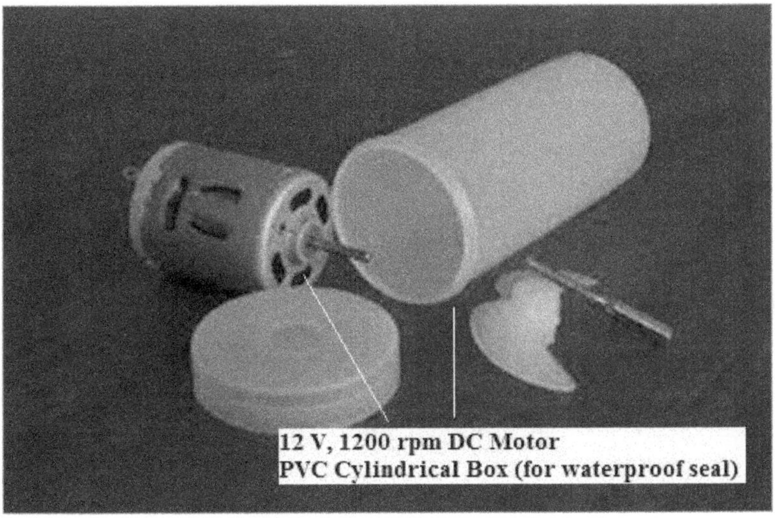

Figure 3.42: Motor with Seal

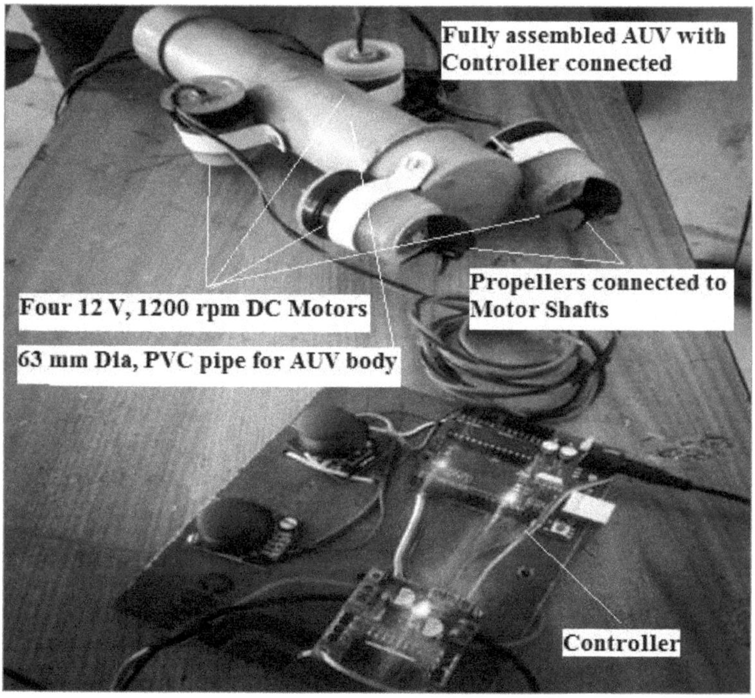

Figure 3.43: Completely Assembled AUV

3. 3 Simulation Techniques

Simulation is used to crosscheck the findings of robot paths acquired via mathematical procedures and experimental testing. For simulation, the Coppelia Robotics® V-REP® tool is used. V-REP® is one of the few user-friendly robot path design simulators available.

3.3.1 V-REP®

V-REP® is a multi-purpose, expansible simulation frame by Copellia Robotics®. By providing a wide range of different programming techniques to its controllers and enabling the integration of controllers and features into models of simulation, it simplifies the work of programmers and reduces the difficulty of deployment to users.

At present, V-REP® has become a widely used and robust controller and simulator robot in academics as well as in the industrial domain. It carries out tasks going from simulation of complex assembly lines in industrial automation applications, algorithm optimization, system verification, robot task planner and controller. The Trajectory/Motion Planning module manages holonomic and non-holonomic trajectory planning tasks for car-like vehicles through a Rapidly exploring Random Tree (RRT) approach. V-REP also supports kinematic chain based path planning tasks.

V-REP is based on a multifaceted design. There is no primary nor central function in V-REP. In contrast, V-REP has a variety of relatively independent features, which can be turned on or off as needed, also on a model basis. Conceptualize a simulation scenario in which a factory robot is picking up packaged boxes and moving them to a different area; V-REP calculates the dynamics for capturing and holding packaged boxes and executes kinematic simulation for other parts of the scene where dynamic effects are insignificant. This technique makes it possible to compute the motion of the factory robot quickly and accurately; that would never be the case if it had been simulated completely using complex dynamic libraries. This kind of hybrid simulation is best for this situation if the robot is rigid and fixed and is not influenced by its surroundings.

Besides tailoring several of its features selectively, V-REP can also use them symbiotically, cooperating with each other. For instance, if the robot is a humanoid, V-REP can deal with leg movements by (a) first compute the inverse kinematics for both legs (i.e. the remaining calculations are automatically carried out. This makes it possible to specify the humanoid movement in a highly versatile manner, as each foot should simply be assigned to follow a 6-dimensional trajectory: the remaining calculations are automatically carried out.

The V-REP robot simulator, with a built-in development environment, is based upon a distributed control architecture: every object or model can be separately controlled via a custom solution, a remote API client or an embedded script. The V-REP is therefore highly versatile and ideal for multi-robot applications. Controllers can be coded in Python, C/C++, Java, Octave or Mat lab.

V-REP is used for industrial automation simulations, rapid algorithm development, teaching robotics, safety double-checking, prototyping and verification, remote monitoring, etc.

For the simulation in V-REP®, the type of robot can be selected from the library. The inputs like starting point, ending point etc., are given using GUI, and the output path is simulated. V-REP® is a path simulation tool used to solve two-dimensional static, two-dimensional dynamic, and three-dimensional static obstacle avoidance issues.

3.3.1.2 Minimum Distance Calculations

V-REP® can quickly calculate the minimum distance between all geometries. i.e., closed or open, concave or convex or any other geometrical collections. The section uses the same data structures as the collision detector module. Further optimization is also carried out with a time coherence caching technique.

3.3.2 V-REP® Setup for AUV

As V-REP® software is not equipped with underwater simulation, an aerial simulation for the equivalent data is computed. As this work is about the path, the results obtained are considered for comparative study.

3.4 Normalization of the Results

A path is a pseudo object representing a succession of points with orientation in space. In navigation, a smoother path is required to reach the endpoint. Parameters like distance, manoeuvring comfort, etc., are associated before selecting a path.

This thesis focuses on finding the length of the path, i.e., the shortest distance between the starting point and the endpoint. In both mathematical calculations and computer simulation techniques, input for the path is given using Cartesian coordinates, where the output result is in terms of a real number. In the experimental setup, care is taken to superimpose the Cartesian coordinate system onto the arena so that results can be converted into real number units. All results mentioned for path lengths are in terms of real numbers.

3.5 Summary

In the present chapter, different methodologies to develop path planning techniques, their benefits and drawbacks, and limits are investigated. New mathematical methodology CCT is designed for robot traversal and obstacle avoidance in a two-dimensional planar arena, passing static elliptical and/or circular obstacles. This procedure, when combined with CRF, discovers a route across mixed elliptical-polygonal obstacles. Dynamic path planning for two mobile robots is given and investigated using the MPD MATLAB® code. SLICE and the 2D3DPP protocol were created to conduct three-dimensional underwater robot route planning. PSO was investigated and used in experiments. V-REP® was used to simulate the routes. These techniques may be extended to incorporate multi-robot operations in multiplex settings, harmonised and networked collective robots of various speeds, creating robots with less payload, and combining classical and reactive approaches. This chapter's shortcoming is that it does not allow you to experiment with and compare the performance of a robot utilising both classical and reactive techniques.

The research's strength is its steadfast adherence to mathematical methodologies and comparable outcomes. CCT and CRF protocols are helpful in creating robots that may be used to clean locations such as vacant classrooms, malls, theatres, parks, industrial workshops, and unmanned warehouses, where the majority of the obstacles are static. MPD performs effectively in home automation robots, hospitality robots, autonomous automobiles, and other similar applications. 2D3DPP and SLICE are ideal for AUVs doing underwater maintenance, surveillance, and reconnaissance in the marine industry. The findings strongly suggest that hybridization is necessary. Robots that use hybrid path planning approaches can provide more advantages in terms of time, money, and risk.

Chapter 4

Two-dimensional Path calculation of a Robot against Static Elliptical Obstacles

In this chapter, various cases for the robot moving on a planar path against elliptical obstacles are tested using a mathematical protocol, a reactive technique based experimentation, and a simulator against the same input conditions. For analytical testing, the 2D3DPP and CCT protocols coded in MATLAB® is called with the input values; numerical and graphical results are plotted.

For experimentation, a reactive method approach is selected. All experiments in this sub-unit have been done on an arena of a 3 m x 3 m white-colour Polyvinyl chloride sheet. Black-colour cardboards are used to make the obstacles. An IR-based sensor is used for obstacle detection, which is connected to an Arduino board. Each experiment has been done three times, and the best path is selected. A scale of 1 Cartesian unit equals 100 mm is used for experimentation. As the robot's imaginary circumscribed circle is 200 mm, the same has been deducted from the obstacles in the lines of configuration space. For simulation, the V-REP® simulator is used.

4.1 Validation of Test Cases

In this chapter, four two-dimensional static test cases (from test case 1 to test case 4) are executed. The obstacles in this chapter are ellipses. All test cases with arbitrary input values are evaluated with classical CCT protocol and V-REP® simulator. The same input values are normalized for a reactive-based experiment. In the first case, the obstacle is a single ellipse, the second and third deal with two ellipses, whereas the fourth is three.

4.2 Test Case 1: In the presence of a Single Elliptical Obstacle

A point robot with the starting point and endpoint coordinates, as mentioned in Table 4.1, encounters an ellipse whose geometrical data is also presented in Table 4.1.

4.2.1 Analytical Solution

Below results are calculated by using 2D3DPP protocol/CCT protocol via code written in MATLAB® with graphical presentation. The graphical results from the

MATLAB® are shown in Figure 4.1 and analytical results in Table 4.2 for right and left paths. The right path result with 6.12 Cartesian units is the best result in this case.

Table 4.1: Input Data for Test Case 1

S No	Robot	Cartesian Units
1	Source (X, Y)	6, 2
2	Destination (X, Y)	3, 7
S No	**Ellipse**	**Cartesian Units**
1	Centre (X, Y)	4, 4.5
2	Major Axis	5
3	Minor Axis	3
4	The inclination of Major Axis with Horizontal in Degrees	-54

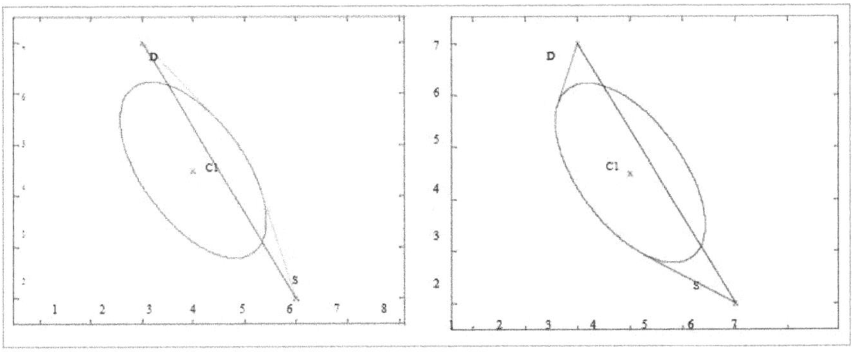

a. Right Path

b. Left Path

Figure 4.1: Graphical Results for Test Case 1

Table 4.2: Analytical Results for Test Case 1

Path obtained from 2D3DPP/CCT Protocol		
Path No.	**Path Direction**	**Length of the Path in Units**
1	Right Path	6.12
2	Left Path	6.90

4.2.2 Experimental Solution

As mentioned in Section 4.1, the experimentation is conducted, and results are tabulated in Table 4.3. A left path with 7.40 Cartesian units is the best of all three iterations. A snapshot of the experiment is presented in Figure 4.2.

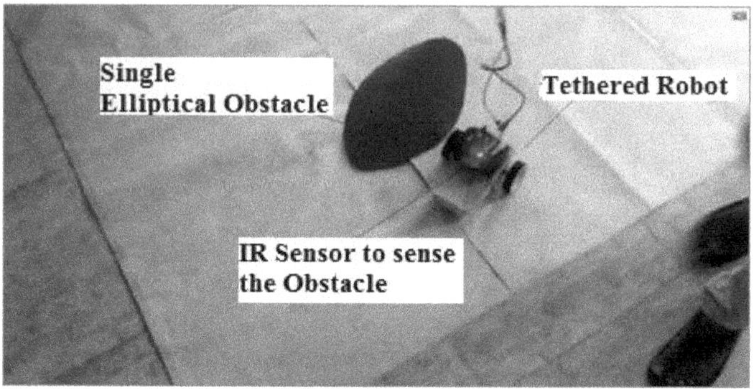

Figure 4.2: Experimental Setup (Single Ellipse)

Table 4.3: Experimental Results for Test Case 1

Path from the Experiment (Reactive Technique Based)		
Iteration No.	**Path Direction**	**Length of the Path normalized to Cartesian Units**
1	Left Path	7.40
2	Left Path	7.43
3	Left Path	7.48

4.2.3 Simulation Solution

A robot with a 2.5 Cartesian unit imaginary circumscribed circle is chosen. Based on configuration space theory, this value is deduced from the obstacles. For the input data mentioned in Table 4.1, the path is generated using V-REP®, and the graphic plot is shown in Figure 4.3. The length of the path obtained from the simulation is 6.30 Units (Left Path).

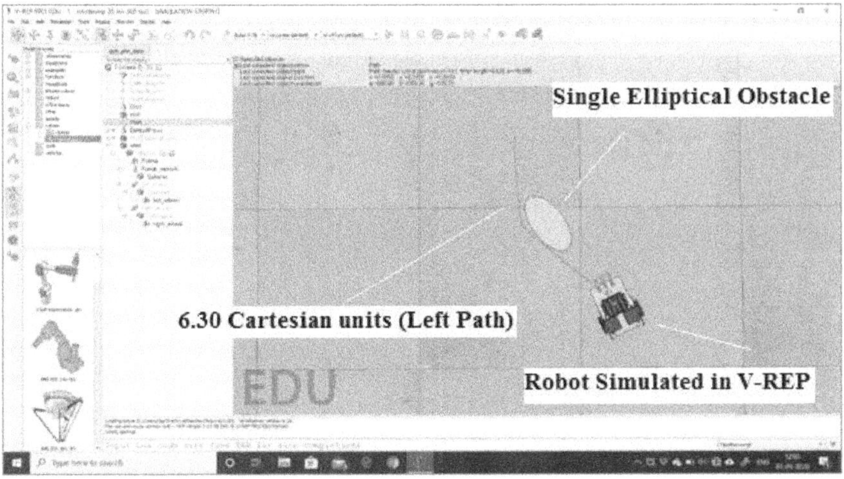

Figure 4.3: V-REP® Simulation Result for Test Case 1

4.3 Test Case 2: In the presence of Two Elliptical Obstacles

For the arbitrary geometrical data, as mentioned in Table 4.4 of two ellipses and a point robot, mathematical protocol, experimentation and simulation is conducted.

4.3.1 Analytical Solution

Results, shown in Table 4.5, are calculated by using 2D3DPP protocol/CCT protocol via code written in MATLAB® with the graphical presentation, Figure 4.4. The right-right path with 28.51 is the optimum distance.

4.3.2 Experimental Solution

The experimentation is conducted, and results are tabulated in Table 4.6. A Right - Right path with 37.40 Cartesian units is the best of all three iterations. Figure 4.5 shows a snapshot of the experiment.

Table 4.4: Input Data for Test Case 2

S No	Robot	Cartesian Units
1	Source (X, Y)	1, 1
2	Destination (X, Y)	20, 20
S No	**Ellipse 1**	**Cartesian Units**
1	Centre (X, Y)	6, 6
2	Major Axis	10
3	Minor Axis	5
4	The inclination of Major Axis with Horizontal in Degrees	-15
S No	**Ellipse 2**	**Cartesian Units**
1	Centre (X, Y)	15, 18
2	Major Axis	10
3	Minor Axis	5
4	The inclination of Major Axis with Horizontal in Degrees	80

Table 4.5: Analytical Results for Test Case 2

Path obtained from 2D3DPP/CCT Protocol		
Path No.	**Path Direction**	**Length of the Path in Units**
1	Left - Left Path	33.07
2	Left - Right Path	30.25
3	Right - Right Path	28.51
4	Right - Left Path	35.51

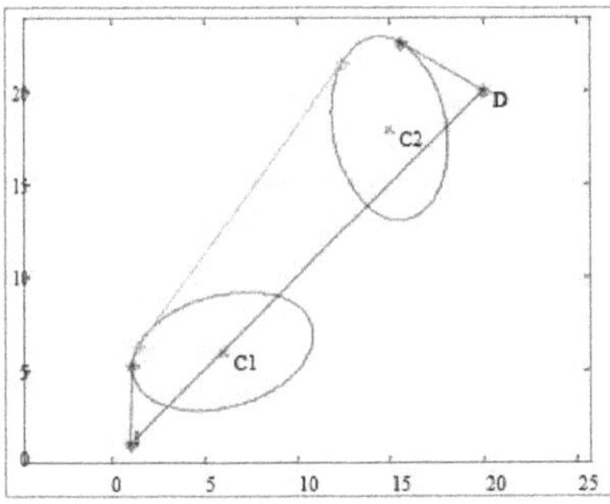

a. Left-Left Path

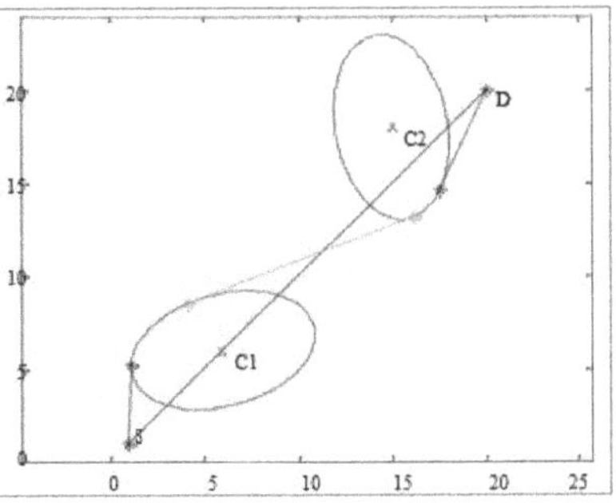

b. Left-Right Path

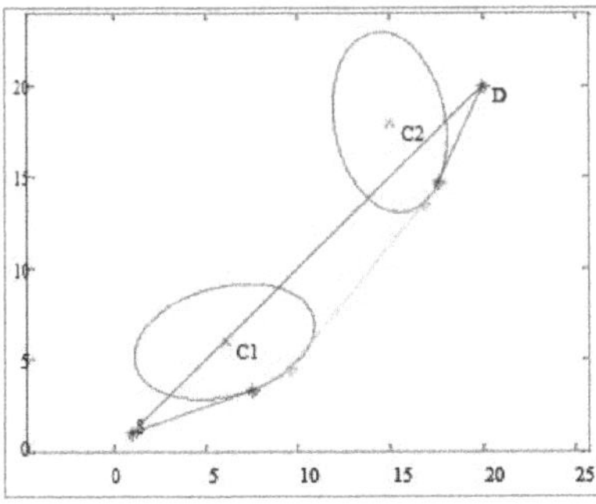

c. Right-Right Path

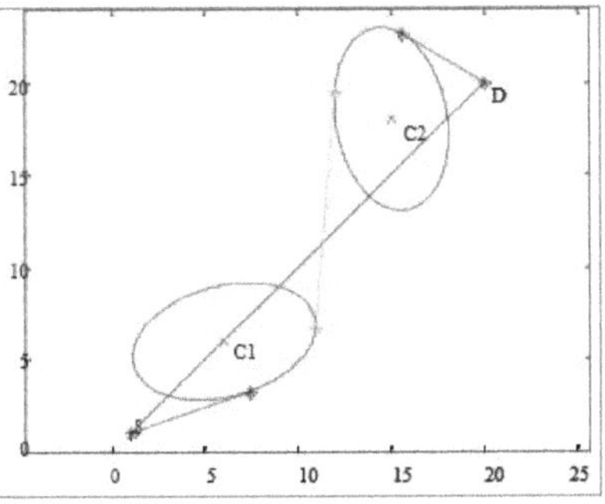

d. Right-Left Path

Figure 4.4: Graphical Results for Test Case 2 (All Four combinations)

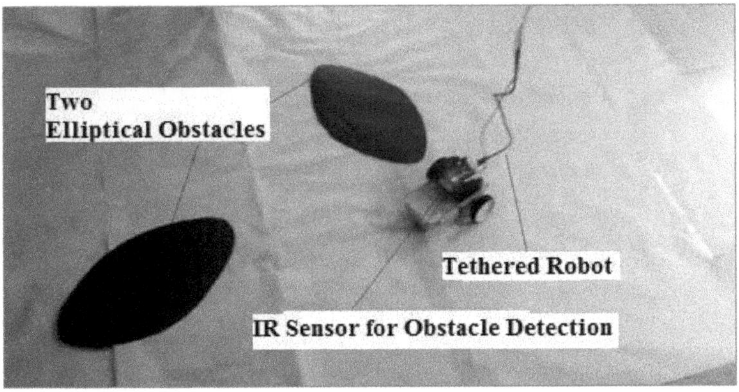

Figure 4.5: Experimental Setup for Test Case 2

Table 4.6: Experimental Results for Test Case 2

Path from the Experiment (Reactive Technique Based)		
Iteration No.	**Path Direction**	**Length of the Path normalized to Cartesian Units**
1	Right-Right Path	37.40
2	Right - Right Path	38.43
3	Right - Right Path	38.48

4.3.3 Simulation Solution

In the lines of configuration space theory, for a robot with a 2.5 Cartesian unit, imaginary circumscribed circle is selected. The same value is subtracted from the obstacles. 29.63 units right-right path is the result obtained through the V-REP® simulator. The graphical path is shown in Figure 4.6

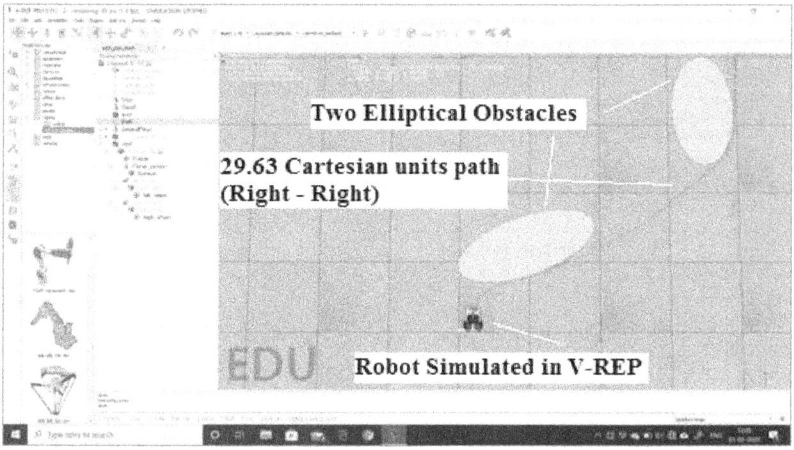

Figure 4.6: V-REP® Simulation Result for Test Case 2

4.4 Test Case 3: In the presence of Two Elliptical Obstacles

The case here is to find the obstacle-free path for a point robot, which avoids collision with two ellipses in its arena. The starting point and endpoint coordinates of the point robot and the geometric details of both the ellipses are presented in Table 4.7.

4.4.1 Analytical Solution

Results, as shown in Table 4.8, are calculated by using 2D3DPP protocol/CCT protocol via code written in MATLAB® with the graphical presentation as shown in Figure 4.7. The left-left path with 29.44 is the optimum distance.

4.4.2 Experimental Solution

The experimental results are tabulated in Table 4.9. A left-left path with 36.80 Cartesian units is the best of all three iterations.

4.4.3 Simulation Solution

The robot is inscribed in an imagined circle of 2.5 Cartesian units. This value is deducted from the obstacles. 31.07 units left-right path is the result obtained through the V-REP® simulator. The graphical path is shown in Figure 4.8.

Table 4.7: Input Data for Test Case 3

S No	Robot	Cartesian Units
1	Source (X, Y)	1, 1
2	Destination (X, Y)	20, 20
S No	**Ellipse 1**	**Cartesian Units**
1	Centre (X, Y)	6, 7
2	Major Axis	10
3	Minor Axis	5
4	The inclination of Major Axis with Horizontal in Degrees	-60
S No	**Ellipse 2**	**Cartesian Units**
1	Centre (X, Y)	15, 4
2	Major Axis	10
3	Minor Axis	5
4	The inclination of Major Axis with Horizontal in Degrees	45

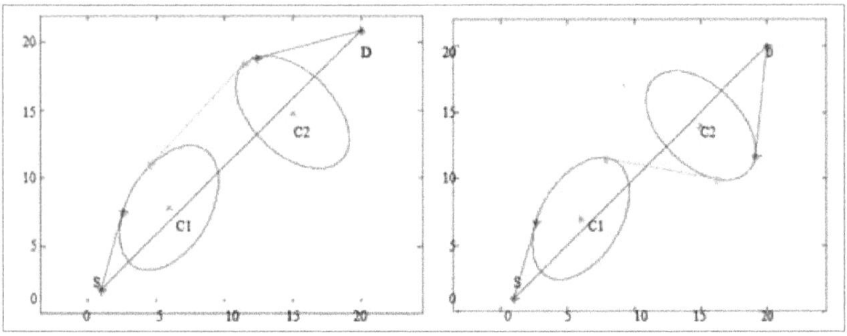

a. Left-Left Path b. Left-Right Path

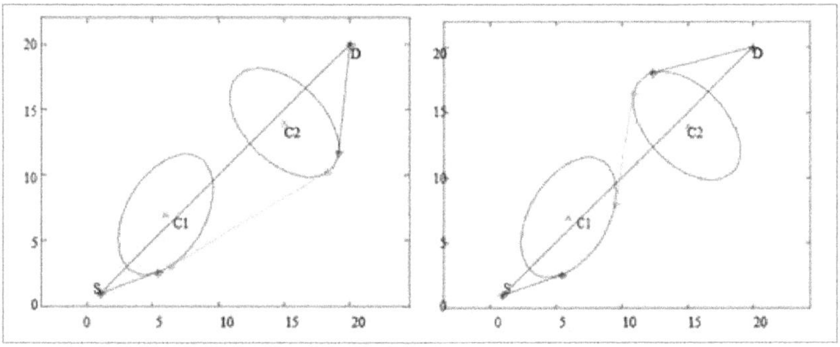

c. Right-Right Path d. Right-Left Path

Figure 4.7: Graphical Results for Test Case 3

Table 4.8: Analytical Results for Test Case 3

Path obtained from 2D3DPP/CCT Protocol		
Path No.	**Path Direction**	**Length of the Path in Units**
1	Left - Left Path	29.44
2	Left - Right Path	34.43
3	Right - Right Path	29.9
4	Right - Left Path	31.07

Table 4.9: Experimental Results for Test Case 3

Path from the Experiment (Reactive Technique Based)		
Iteration No.	**Path Direction**	**Length of the Path normalized to Cartesian Units**
1	Right - Left Path	38.46
2	Right - Right Path	36.96
3	Left - Left Path	36.80

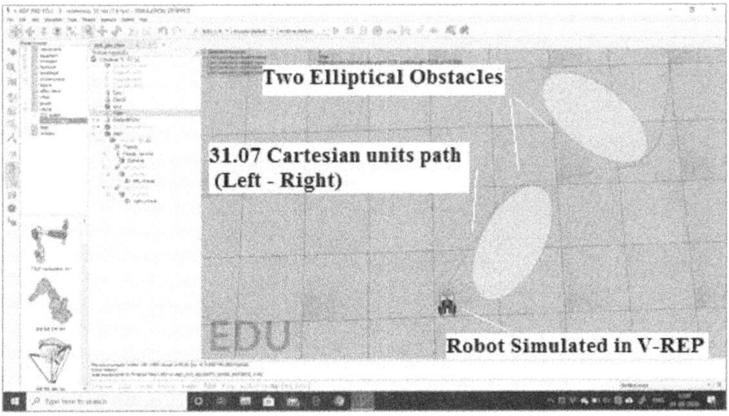

Figure 4.8: V-REP® Simulation Result for Test Case 3

4.5 Test Case 4: In the presence of Three Elliptical Obstacles

Table 4.10 shows the input data for a point robot and three ellipses. For the robot, the starting point and endpoint positions are fixed arbitrarily, and for ellipses, the centre point, axes lengths and inclination with the horizontal.

4.5.1 Analytical Solution

By using mathematical protocols, results are calculated. The graphical results are shown in Figures 4.9 and 4.10. Table 4.11 is the input data, and Table 4.12 is the output analytical data.

Table 4.10: Input Data for Test Case 4

S No	Robot	Cartesian Units
1	Source (X, Y)	4, 7
2	Destination (X, Y)	17, 15
S No	**Ellipse 1**	**Cartesian Units**
1	Centre (X, Y)	7, 8
2	Major Axis	4
3	Minor Axis	3
4	The inclination of Major Axis with Horizontal in Degrees	0
S No	**Ellipse 2**	**Cartesian Units**
1	Centre (X, Y)	10.5, 10.5
2	Major Axis	6
3	Minor Axis	3
4	The inclination of Major Axis with Horizontal in Degrees	0
S No	**Ellipse 3**	**Cartesian Units**
1	Centre (X, Y)	15, 13.5
2	Major Axis	4
3	Minor Axis	3
4	The inclination of Major Axis with Horizontal in Degrees	1

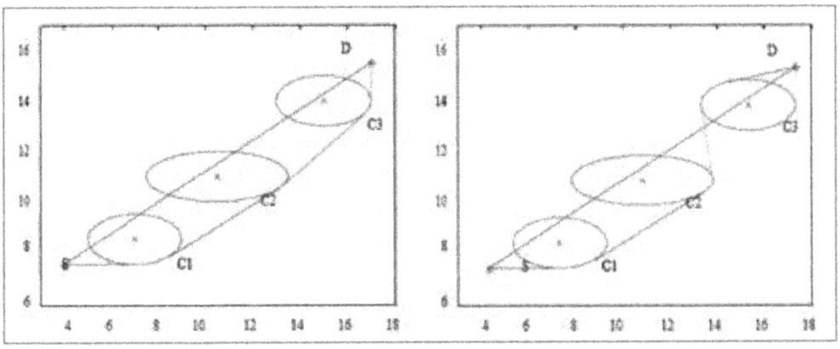

a. Right-Right-Right Path b. Right-Right-Left Path

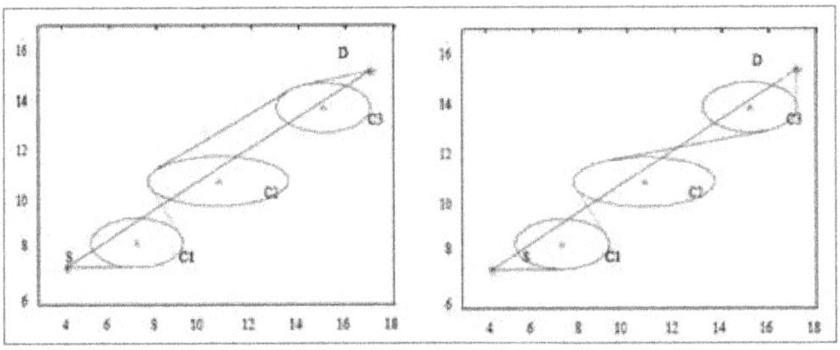

c. Right-Left-Left Path d. Right-Left-Right Path

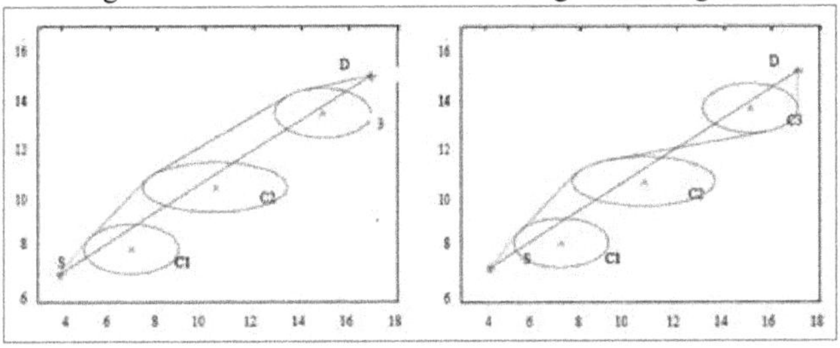

e. Left-Left-Left Path f. Left-Left-Right Path

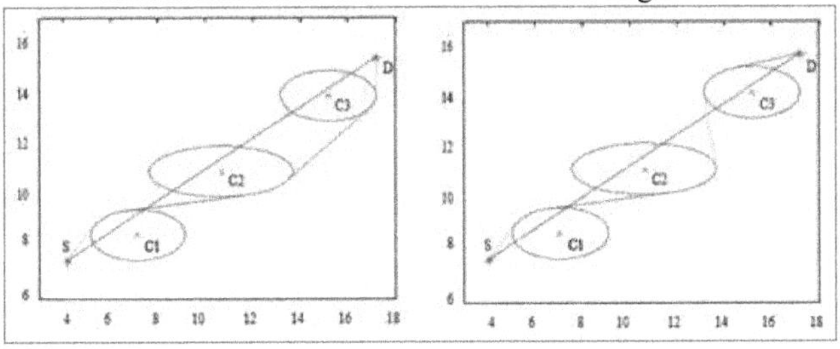

g. Left-Right-Right Path h. Left-Right-Left Path

Figure 4.9: Graphical Results for Test Case 4

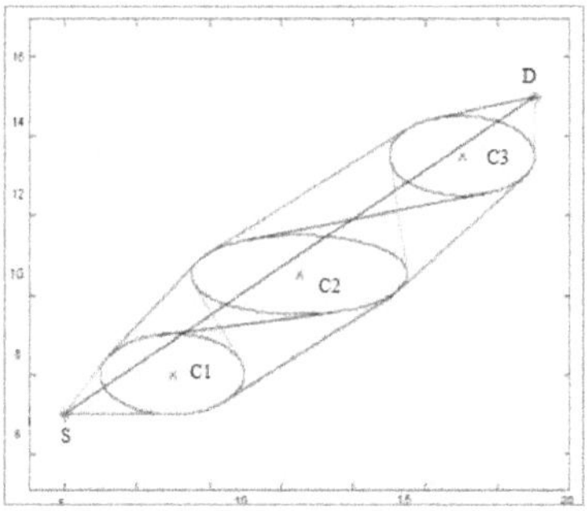

Figure 4.10: Combined Graphical Results for Test Case 4 (All eight combinations)

Table 4.11: Analytical Results for Test Case 4

Path obtained from 2D3DPP/CCT Protocol		
Path No.	**Path Direction**	**Length of the Path in Units**
1	Right-Right-Right Path	16.89
2	Right-Right-Left Path	18.28
3	Right-Left-Left Path	18.92
4	Right-Left-Right Path	20.02
5	Left- Left-Left Path	17.76
6	Left-Left-Right Path	19.62
7	Left-Right-Right Path	17.17
8	Left-Right-Left Path	18.45

The right-right-right path with 16.89 is the optimum distance.

4.5.2 Experimental Solution

With three elliptical patches as obstacles on a vinyl sheet for a robot is established as per the normalized coordinates. The experimentation is conducted, and results are tabulated in Table 4.12. A left-left path with 20.21 Cartesian units is the best of all three iterations. The experimental setup is similar to two ellipses as in Test Case 2.

4.5.4 Simulation Solution

18.89 units left-left-right path is the result obtained through the V-REP® simulator. The graphical path is shown in Figure 4.11.

Table 4.12: Experimental Results for Test Case 4

Path from the Experiment (Reactive Technique Based)		
Iteration No.	**Path Direction**	**Length of the Path normalized to Cartesian Units**
1	Left-Left-Left Path	23.24
2	Right-Left-Right Path	22.46
3	Left-Left-Left Path	20.21

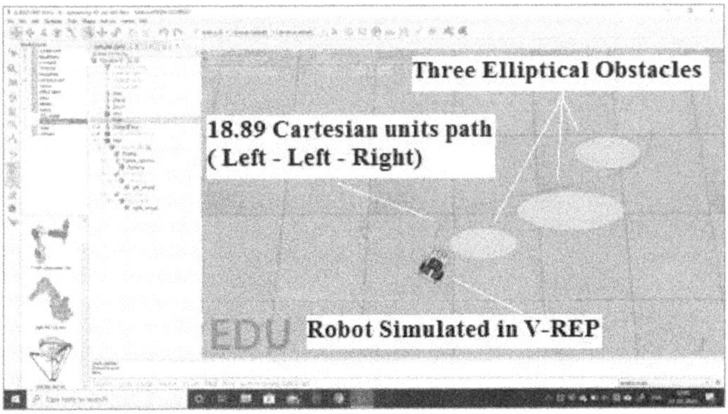

Figure 4.11: V-REP® Simulation Result for Test Case 4

4.6 Summary

A new mathematical methodology CCT is evaluated in a two-dimensional planar arena for robot traversal and obstacle avoidance while crossing static elliptical and/or circular obstacles. A reactive approach is utilised to compute the route empirically. The results of this chapter may be applied to static barriers of any shape or size. This chapter's shortcoming is that it does not test a robot's performance for varied curvature form obstacles. The chapter's research strength is the common tangent method between two ellipses. This method may be used to mobile gaming. The chapter study strongly suggests that common tangents be found for every type of curvature-based form.

4.7 Conclusions

In this chapter, four test cases (Test Case 1 - 4) for finding collision-free paths for robots in the presence of one/two/three ellipses as obstacles are presented. From the results obtained from the analytical, experimental and simulation methods, it is observed that analytical solutions are providing minimum distance paths, and experimental results are giving maximum distance paths. It is also observed that the increase of path distances of experimental results above the analytical solutions varies between 18 % to 32 %, as shown in Table 4.13. The experimental technique is based on IR obstacle detection. The algorithms described above use computational geometry to compute the shortest distance in the analytical findings. The reaction time of the sensor used, the response time of the actuator motor, the shape, size, orientation and number of ellipses are the causes for the % increase in experimentation. The path distances obtained in V-Rep® simulator are more by around 2% to 12 % over analytical solutions because of the proprietary reactive algorithms of the simulator, the configuration space and geometry of the obstacles.

Table 4.13: Comparative Table for Test Cases 1- 4

Test Case	Test Case Description		Mathematical (Classical) Protocol Used and Path obtained		Path obtained from Reactive Technique based Experiment	Path obtained from the V-REP®	% Increase for Experiment over Analytical	% Increase for Simulation over Analytical
	Robot Description	Obstacle Description						
1	A robot moving in a two-dimensional planar arena	The obstacle is a single ellipse	2D3DPP / CCT	6.12	7.40	6.30	20.92	2.94
2		Two elliptical obstacles in the robot's path	2D3DPP / CCT	28.51	37.40	29.63	31.18	3.93
3			2D3DPP / CCT	29.44	36.80	31.07	25.00	5.54
4		Robot encounters three ellipses	2D3DPP / CCT	16.89	20.21	18.89	19.66	11.84

Chapter 5

Two-dimensional Path calculation of a Robot against Static Mixed Obstacles

In this chapter, various cases for the robot moving on a planar path against the combination of elliptical, circular and polygonal obstacles are tested using the mathematical protocol, experimentation, and simulation against the same input conditions. For analytical testing, the 2D3DPP protocol coded in MATLAB® is called with the input values, and numerical and graphical results are plotted. CCT and CRF protocols are the sub-routines of the 2D3DPP protocol.

A reactive method approach is used for experimentation. All tests in this sub-unit were conducted on a 3 m × 3 m white Polyvinyl chloride sheet arena. The barriers are made of black-coloured cardboard. For obstacle detection, an IR-based sensor linked to an Arduino board is utilised. Each experiment has been repeated three times, and the optimal path has been chosen. For experimentation, a scale of 1 Cartesian unit = 100 mm is employed. Because the imaginary circumscribed circle of the robot is 200 mm, the obstacles are adjusted as per configuration space theory. The experimental setup is similar to two ellipses as in Test Case 2. The V-REP® simulator is used for simulation.

5.1 Validation of Test Cases

This chapter executes seven test cases (5 to 11). The robot's two-dimensional path is calculated against static obstacles. This chapter's obstacles are made out of ellipses, circles, and polygons. The classical CCT protocol and the V-REP® simulator assess all test cases with arbitrary input values. For a reactive-based experiment, the identical input data is normalized. Test cases are as follows: ellipse-polygon, polygon-ellipse, polygon-circle, polygon-polygon-circle, polygon-polygon-ellipse, circle-ellipse-polygon, ellipse-polygon-ellipse.

5.2 Test Case 5: In the presence of an Ellipse and a Polygon

A point robot with the starting point and endpoint coordinates, as mentioned in Table 5.1, encounters the obstacles of an ellipse and a polygon, whose geometrical data is also presented in Table 5.1.

Table 5.1: Input Data for Test Case 5

S No	Robot	Cartesian Units
1	Source (X, Y)	2, 13
2	Destination (X, Y)	17, 11
S No	**Ellipse**	**Cartesian Units**
1	Centre (X, Y)	8, 12
2	Major Axis	5
3	Minor Axis	3
4	The inclination of Major Axis with Horizontal in Degrees	15
S No	**Polygon**	**Cartesian Units**
1	V1 (X, Y)	13, 11
2	V2 (X, Y)	15, 9
3	V3 (X, Y)	17, 12
4	V4 (X, Y)	19, 10
5	V5 (X, Y)	17, 16
6	V6 (X, Y)	15, 13
7	V7 (X, Y)	13, 13

5.2.1 Analytical Solution

Below results are calculated by using 2D3DPP protocol/CCT and CRF protocol via code written in MATLAB® with graphical presentation. The graphical results from the MATLAB® are shown in Figure 5.1 and analytical results in Table 5.2 for right and left paths. The left-right path result with 17.94 Cartesian units is the best result in this case.

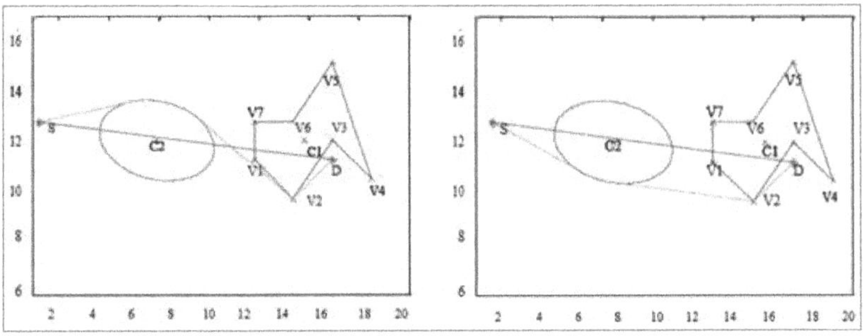

a. Left-Right Path b. Right-Right Path

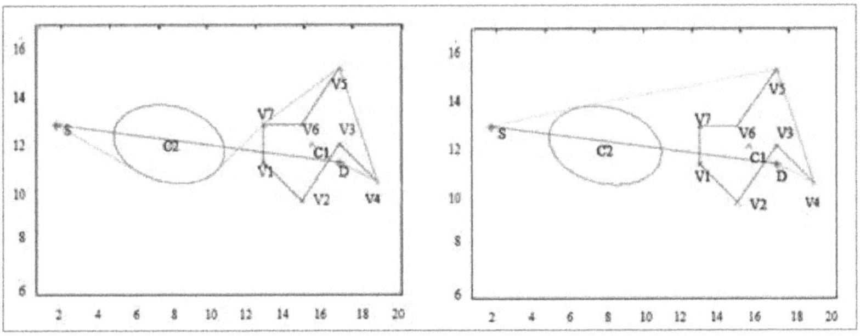

c. Right-Left Path d. Left-Left Path

Figure 5.1: Graphical Results for Test Case 5

Table 5.2: Analytical Results for Test Case 5

Path obtained from 2D3DPP/CCT and CRF Protocol		
Path No.	**Path Direction**	**Length of the Path in Units**
1	Left-Right Path	17.94
2	Right-Right Path	19.81
3	Right-Left Path	26.68
4	Left-Left Path	23.86

5.2.2 Experimental Solution

As mentioned in Section 5.1, on the arena established, the experimentation is conducted, and results are tabulated in Table 5.3. A right-right path with 22.46 Cartesian units is the best of all three iterations.

Table 5.3: Experimental Results for Test Case 5

Path from the Experiment (Reactive Technique Based)		
Iteration No.	**Path Direction**	**Length of the Path normalized to Cartesian Units**
1	Right-Right Path	24.78
2	Right-Right Path	27.24
3	Right-Right Path	22.46

5.2.3 Simulation Solution

For the input data mentioned in Table 5.1, the path is generated using V-REP®, and the graphic plot is shown in Figure 5.2. The length of the path obtained from the simulation is 18.47 Units (Left-Right Path).

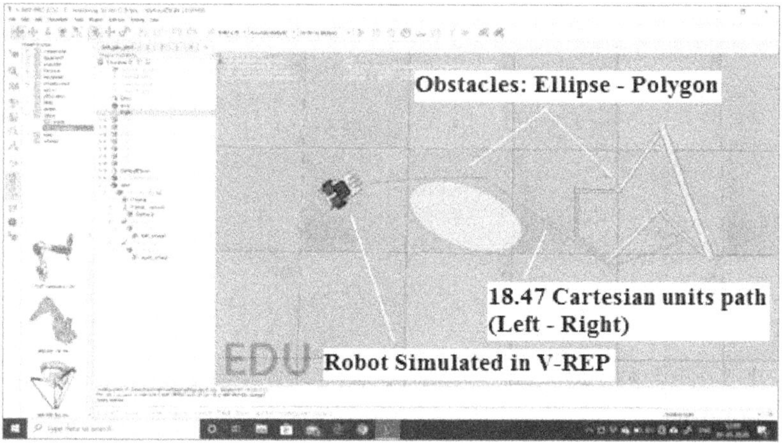

Figure 5.2: V-REP® Simulation Result for Test Case 5

5.3 Test Case 6: In the presence of a Polygon and an Elliptical Obstacle

For the arbitrary geometrical data, as mentioned in Table 5.4 for a polygonal and an elliptical obstacle and a point robot, the mathematical, experimental and simulation solution is calculated.

Table 5.4: Input Data for Test Case 6

S No	Robot	Cartesian Units
1	Source (X, Y)	1, 1
2	Destination (X, Y)	14, 6
S No	**Ellipse**	**Cartesian Units**
1	Centre (X, Y)	10, 13
2	Major Axis	5
3	Minor Axis	3
4	The inclination of Major Axis with Horizontal in Degrees	79
S No	**Polygon**	**Cartesian Units**
1	V1 (X, Y)	6, 3
2	V2 (X, Y)	8, 4
3	V3 (X, Y)	9, 6
4	V4 (X, Y)	8, 8
5	V5 (X, Y)	5, 8
6	V6 (X, Y)	4, 5

5.3.1 Analytical Solution

Results, shown in Table 5.5, are calculated by using 2D3DPP protocol/CCT/CRF protocols via code written in MATLAB® with the graphical presentation, Figure 5.3. The left-right path with 20.29 is the optimum distance.

Table 5.5: Analytical Results for Test Case 6

Path obtained from 2D3DPP/CCT and CRF Protocol		
Path No.	**Path Direction**	**Length of the Path in Units**
1	Left - Left Path	21.10
2	Left - Right Path	20.29
3	Right - Right Path	20.77
4	Right - Left Path	24.75

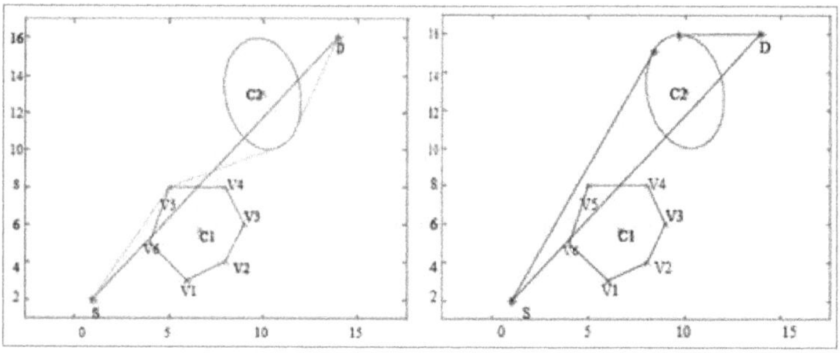

a. Left-Right Path b. Left-Left Path

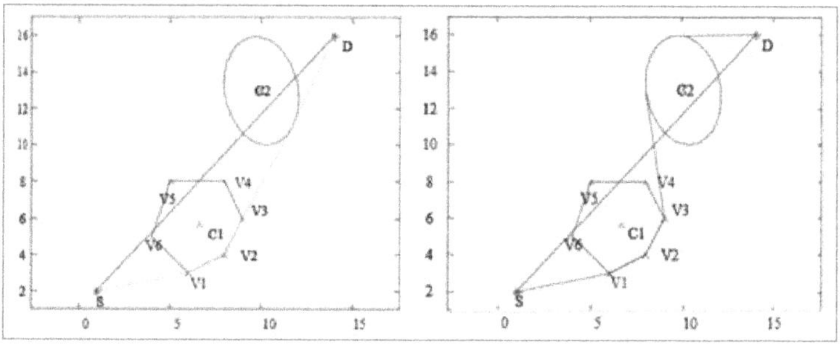

c. Right-Right Path d. Right-Left Path

Figure 5.3: Graphical Results for Test Case 6

5.3.2 Experimental Solution

The experimentation is conducted, and results are tabulated in Table 5.6. A left-left path with 26.36 Cartesian units is the best of all three iterations.

Table 5.6: Experimental Results for Test Case 6

Path from the Experiment (Reactive Technique Based)		
Iteration No.	**Path Direction**	**Length of the Path normalized to Cartesian Units**
1	Left - Left Path	27.42
2	Left - Left Path	26.36
3	Left - Left Path	28.97

5.3.3 Simulation Solution

23.46 units left-left path is the result obtained through the V-REP® simulator. The graphical path is shown in Figure 5.4.

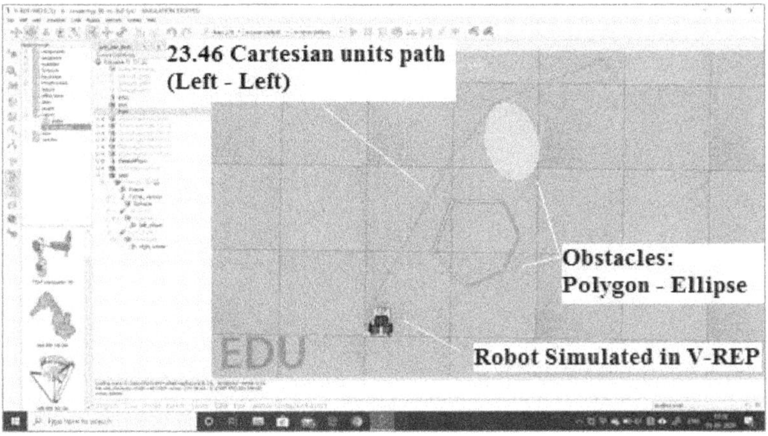

Figure 5.4: V-REP® Simulation Result for Test Case 6

5.4 Test Case 7: In the presence of a Polygon and a Circle

The case here is to find the obstacle-free path for a point robot around a polygon and a circle. The starting point and endpoint coordinates of the point robot and the geometric details of the polygon and the circle are presented in Table 5.7.

5.4.1 Analytical Solution

Results, as shown in Table 5.8, are calculated by using 2D3DPP/CRF/CCT protocols via code written in MATLAB® with the graphical presentation, as shown in the Figures 5.5 and 5.6, the right-right path with 20.65 is the optimum distance.

5.4.2 Experimental Solution

The experimental results are tabulated in Table 5.9. A right-right path with 27.20 Cartesian units is the best of all three iterations.

Table 5.7: Input Data for Test Case 7

S No	Robot	Cartesian Units
1	Source (X, Y)	1, 2
2	Destination (X, Y)	14, 16
S No	**Circle**	**Cartesian Units**
1	Centre (X, Y)	10, 12
2	Diameter	5
S No	**Polygon**	**Cartesian Units**
1	V1 (X, Y)	6, 3
2	V2 (X, Y)	6, 8
3	V3 (X, Y)	2, 8
4	V4 (X, Y)	2, 3

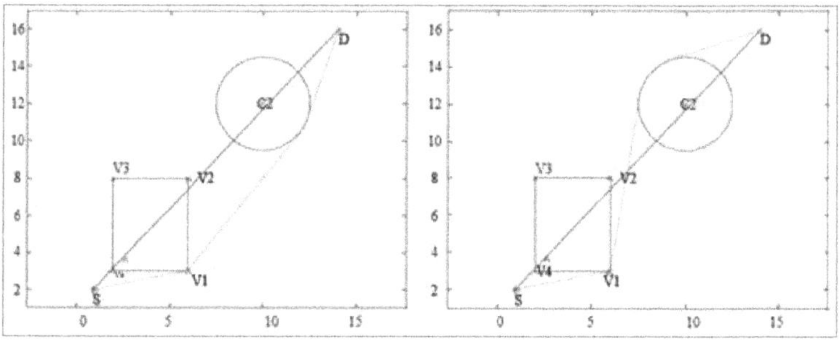

a. Right-Right Path

b. Right-Left Path

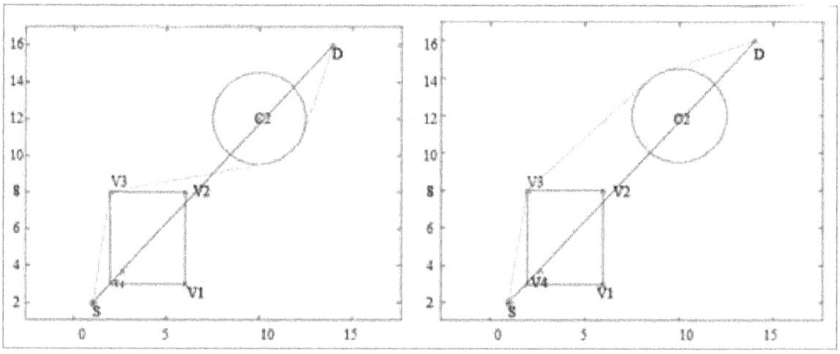

c. Left-Right Path

d. Left-Left Path

Figure 5.5: Graphical Results for Test Case 7

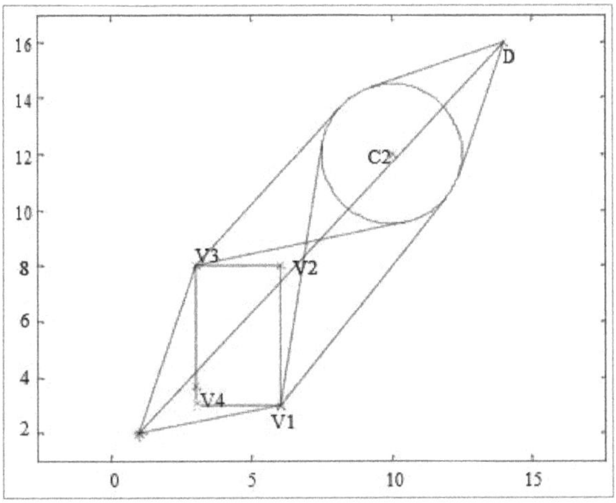

Figure 5.6: Graphical Results for Test Case 7 (All four combinations)

Table 5.8: Analytical Results for Test Case 7

Path obtained from 2D3DPP/CCT and CRF Protocol		
Path No.	**Path Direction**	**Length of the Path in Units**
1	Left - Left Path	24.84
2	Left - Right Path	24.65
3	Right - Right Path	20.65
4	Right - Left Path	22.55

Table 5.9: Experimental Results for Test Case 7

Path from the Experiment (Reactive Technique Based)		
Iteration No.	**Path Direction**	**Length of the Path normalized to Cartesian Units**
1	Right - Right Path	28.46
2	Right - Right Path	29.15
3	Right - Right Path	27.20

5.4.3 Simulation Solution

23.58 units right-right path is the result obtained through the V-REP® simulator. The graphical path is shown in Figure 5.7.

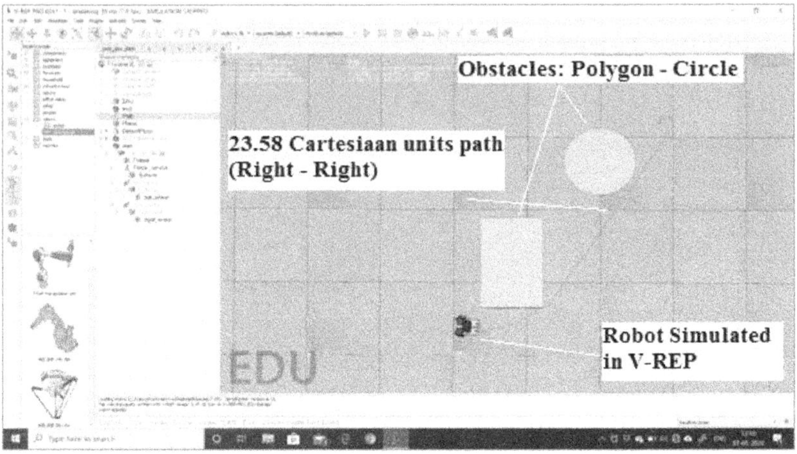

Figure 5.7: V-REP® Simulation Result for Test Case 7

5.5 Test Case 8: In the presence of Two Polygonal and a Circular Obstacle

Table 5.10 shows the input data for a point robot with two polygons and a circle. The robot starting and ending point, vertices of the polygons and centre-radius of the circle are fixed arbitrarily.

5.5.1 Analytical Solution

By using mathematical protocols, results are calculated. The graphical results are shown in Figures 5.8 and 5.9. Table 5.10 is the input data, and Table 5.11 is the output analytical data.

5.5.2 Experimental Solution

With two polygonal and one circular patch as obstacles on a vinyl sheet for a robot is established as per the normalized coordinates. The experimentation is conducted, and results are tabulated in Table 5.12. A left-left-left path with 30.42 Cartesian units is the best of all three iterations.

Table 5.10: Input Data for Test Case 8

S No	Robot	Cartesian Units
1	Source (X, Y)	3, 3
2	Destination (X, Y)	23, 16
S No	**Circle**	**Cartesian Units**
1	Centre (X, Y)	19, 12
2	Diameter	5
S No	**Polygon 1**	**Cartesian Units**
1	V1 (X, Y)	5, 4.5
2	V2 (X, Y)	5, 6
3	V3 (X, Y)	7, 6
4	V4 (X, Y)	7, 5
5	V5 (X, Y)	9, 5
6	V6 (X, Y)	9, 6
7	V7 (X, Y)	11, 6
8	V8 (X, Y)	11, 4.5
S No	**Polygon 2**	**Cartesian Units**
1	V1 (X, Y)	13, 7.5
2	V2 (X, Y)	15, 8.5
3	V3 (X, Y)	17, 8
4	V4 (X, Y)	16, 10
5	V5 (X, Y)	14, 10.5
6	V6 (X, Y)	11, 9

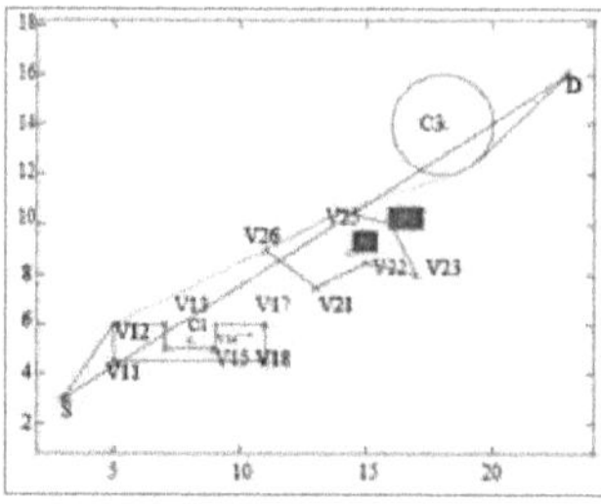

a. Left-Left-Right Path

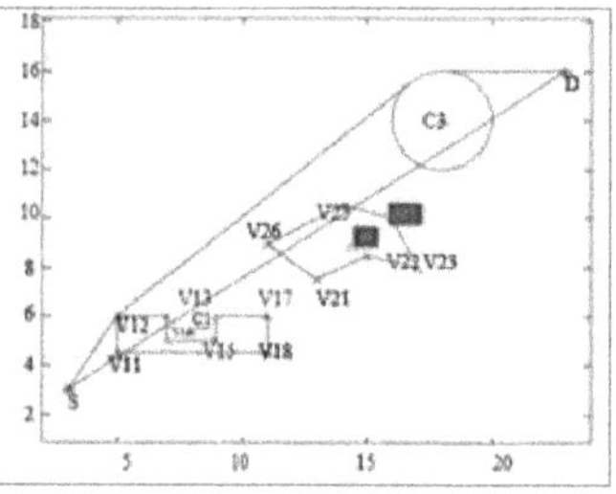

b. Left-Left-Left Path

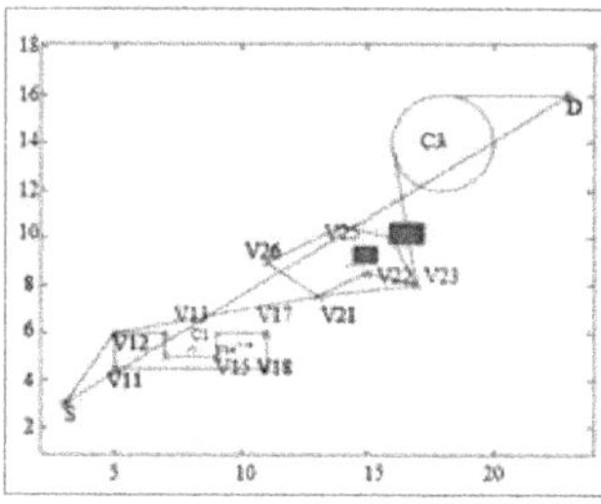

c. Left-Right-Left Path

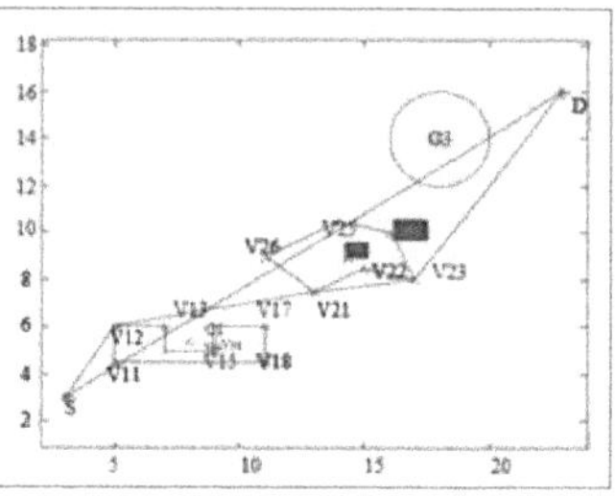

d. Left-Right-Right Path

Figure 5.8: Graphical Results for Test Case 8 (Part A)

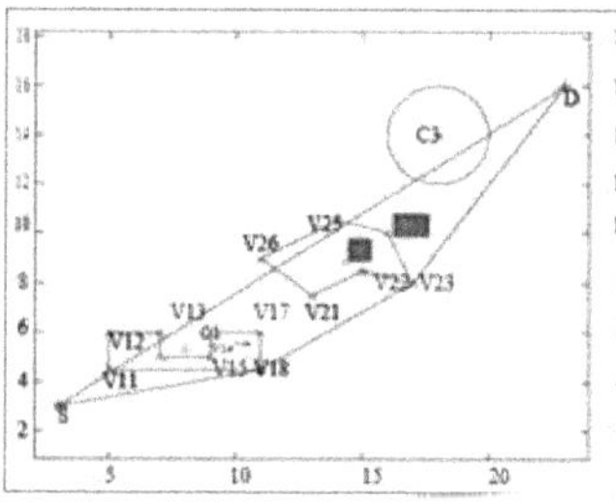

a. Right-Right-Right Path

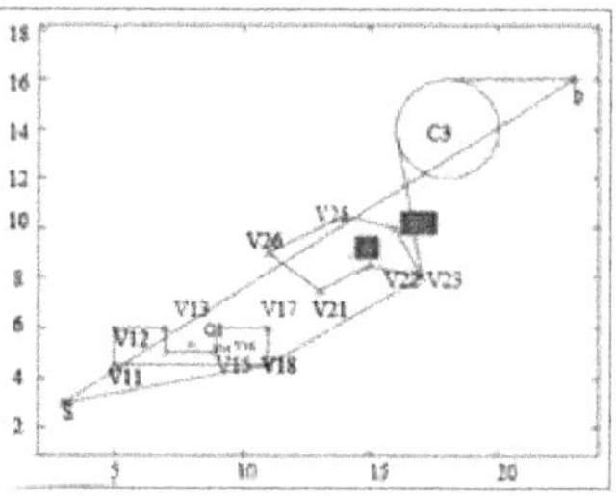

b. Right-Right-Left Path

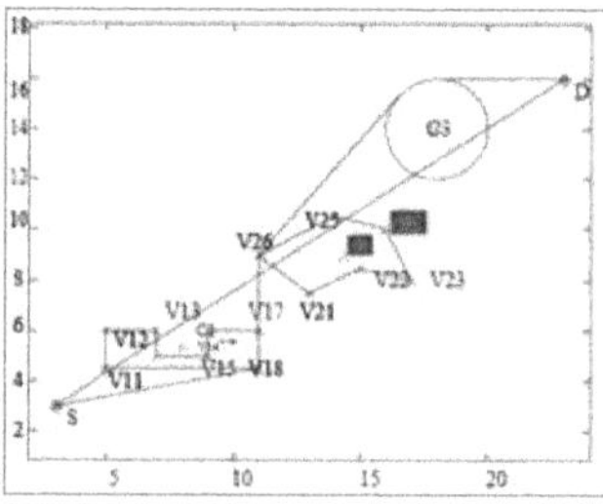

c. Right-Left-Left Path

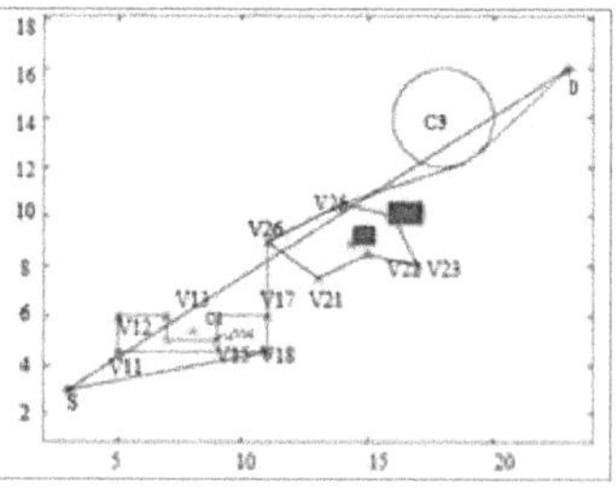

d. Right-Left-Right Path

Figure 5.9: Graphical Results for Test Case 8 (Part B)

Table 5.11: Analytical Results for Test Case 8

Path obtained from 2D3DPP/CCT and CRF Protocol		
Path No.	**Path Direction**	**Length of the Path in Units**
1	Right-Right-Right Path	25.08
2	Right-Right-Left Path	31.51
3	Right-Left-Left Path	26.72
4	Right-Left-Right Path	29.09
5	Left- Left-Left Path	24.32
6	Left-Left-Right Path	27.93
7	Left-Right-Right Path	25.77
8	Left-Right-Left Path	32.20

The left-left-left path with 24.32 is the optimum distance.

Table 5.12: Experimental Results for Test Case 8

Path from the Experiment (Reactive Technique Based)		
Iteration No.	**Path Direction**	**Length of the Path normalized to Cartesian Units**
1	Left-Left-Left Path	30.46
2	Right-Left-Right Path	32.47
3	Left-Left-Left Path	30.42

5.5.3 Simulation Solution

27.46 units left-left-left path is the result obtained through the V-REP® simulator. The graphical path is shown in Figure 5.10.

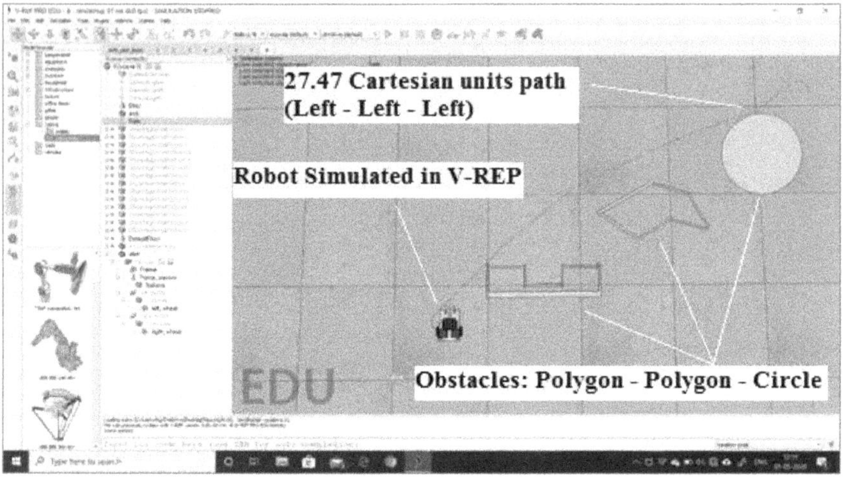

Figure 5.10: V-REP® Simulation Result for Test Case 8

5.6 Test Case 9: In the presence of Two Polygonal and an Elliptical Obstacle

Table 5.13 shows the input data for a point robot with two polygons and an ellipse. The robot starting and ending point, vertices of the polygons and data for the ellipses are fixed arbitrarily.

5.6.1 Analytical Solution

By using mathematical protocols CCT and CRF, results are calculated. The graphical results are shown in Figures 5.11 and 5.12. For Table 5.13 input data, Table 5.14 projects the output analytical data. 24.90 left-left-left is the optimum path.

5.6.2 Experimental Solution

The point robot avoids collision against two polygonal and an elliptical patch. The experimentation is conducted as mentioned in 5.1, and results are tabulated in Table 5.15. A right-right-right path of 29.46 Cartesian units is the best of all three iterations.

Table 5.13: Input Data for Test Case 9

S No	Robot	Cartesian Units
1	Source (X, Y)	3, 3
2	Destination (X, Y)	23, 6
S No	**Ellipse**	**Cartesian Units**
1	Centre (X, Y)	19, 12
2	Major Axis	5
3	Minor Axis	3
4	The inclination of Major Axis with Horizontal in Degrees	56
S No	**Polygon 1**	**Cartesian Units**
1	V1 (X, Y)	5, 4.5
2	V2 (X, Y)	5, 6
3	V3 (X, Y)	7, 6
4	V4 (X, Y)	7, 5
5	V5 (X, Y)	9, 5
6	V6 (X, Y)	9, 6
7	V7 (X, Y)	11, 6
8	V8 (X, Y)	11, 4.5
S No	**Polygon 2**	**Cartesian Units**
1	V1 (X, Y)	14, 6
2	V2 (X, Y)	7, 7
3	V3 (X, Y)	14, 12
4	V4 (X, Y)	11, 11

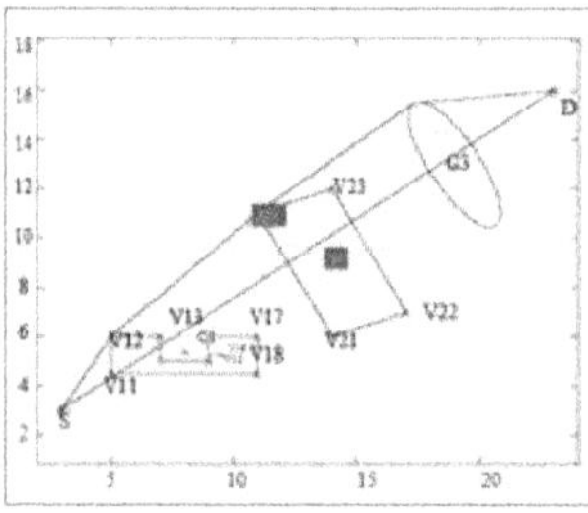

a. Left-Left-Left Path

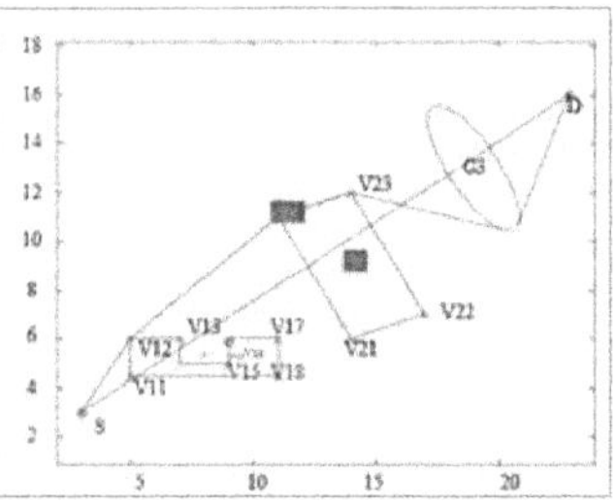

b. Left-Left-Right Path

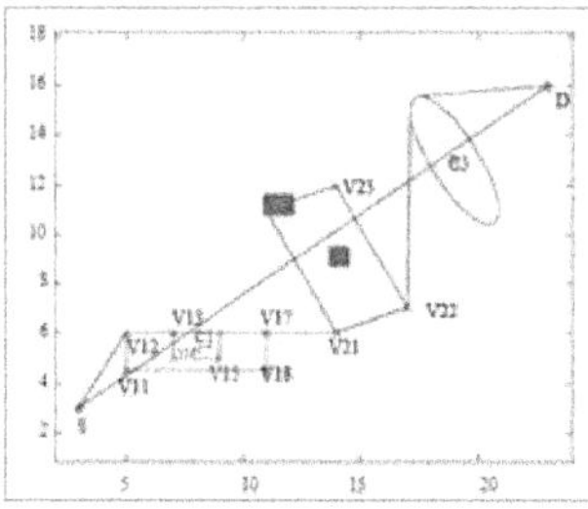

c. Left-Right-Left Path

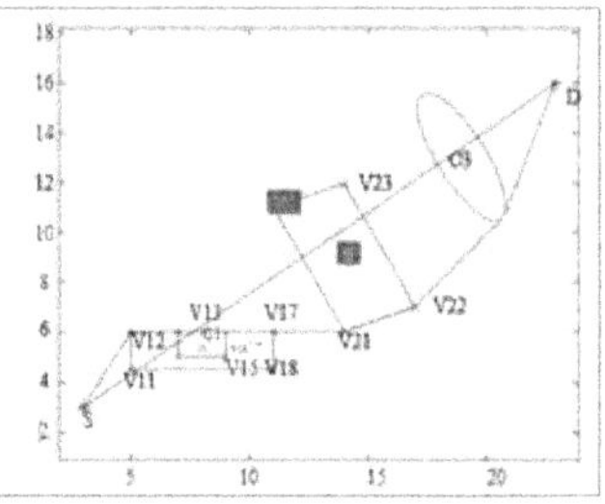

d. Left-Right-Right Path

Figure 5.11: Graphical Results for Test Case 9 (Part A)

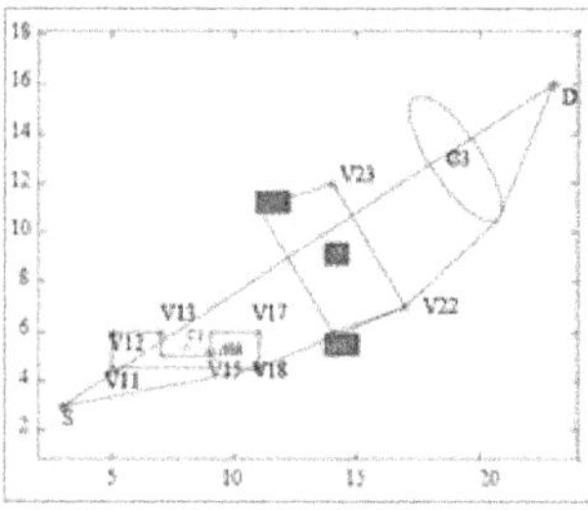

a. Right-Right-Right Path

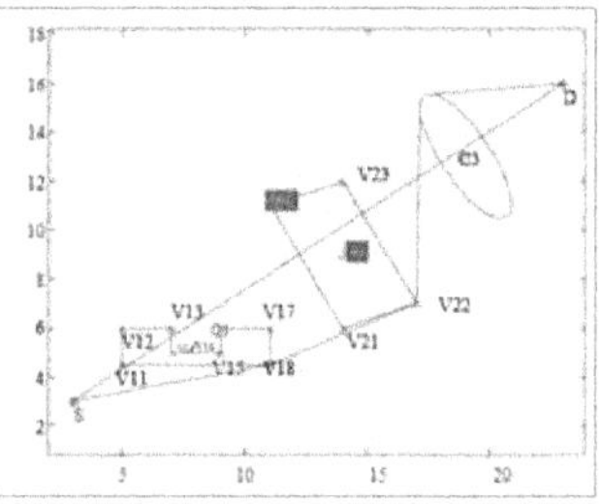

b. Right-Right-Left Path

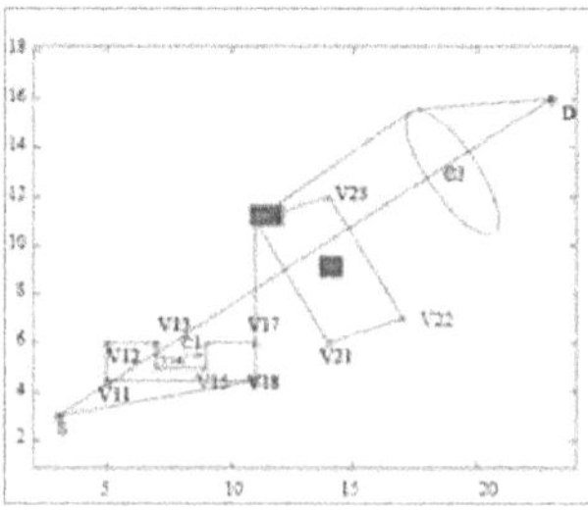

c. Right-Left-Left Path

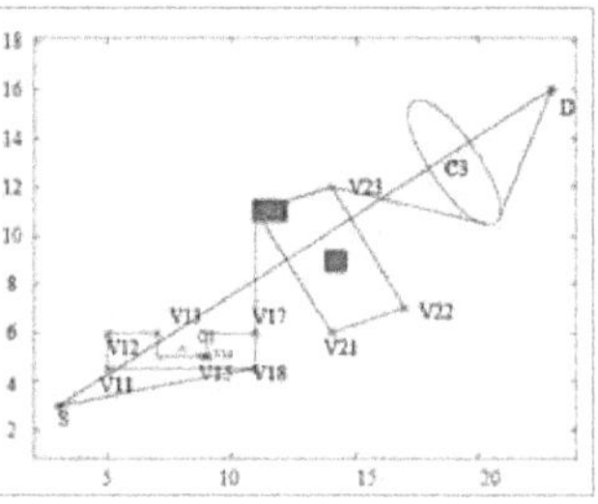

d. Right-Left-Right Path

Figure 5.12: Graphical Results for Test Case 9 (Part B)

Table 5.14: Analytical Results for Test Case 9

Path obtained from 2D3DPP/CCT and CRF Protocol		
Path No.	**Path Direction**	**Length of the Path in Units**
1	Right-Right-Right Path	25.71
2	Right-Right-Left Path	28.82
3	Right-Left-Left Path	34.71
4	Right-Left-Right Path	30.64
5	Left- Left-Left Path	24.90
6	Left-Left-Right Path	27.20
7	Left-Right-Right Path	26.84
8	Left-Right-Left Path	30.02

Table 5.15: Experimental Results for Test Case 9

Path from the Experiment (Reactive Technique Based)		
Iteration No.	**Path Direction**	**Length of the Path normalized to Cartesian Units**
1	Right-Right-Right Path	29.46
2	Right-Right-Right Path	30.42
3	Right-Right-Right Path	29.81

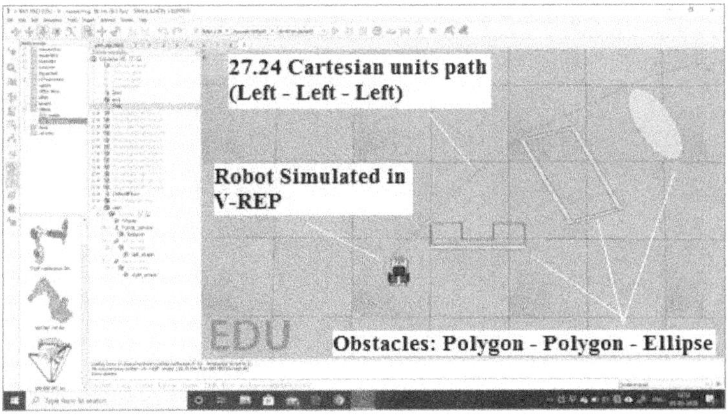

Figure 5.13: Simulation Path for Test Case 9

5.6.3 Simulation Solution

27.24 units left-left-left path is the result obtained through the V-REP® simulator. The graphical path is shown in Figure 5.13.

5.7 Test Case 10: Obstacles: A Circle, an Ellipse and a Polygon

Table 5.16 shows the input data for a point robot with two polygons and an ellipse. The robot starting and ending point, vertices of the polygons and data for the ellipses are fixed arbitrarily.

Table 5.16: Input Data for Test Case 10

S No	Robot	Cartesian Units
1	Source (X, Y)	1, 2
2	Destination (X, Y)	22, 19
S No	**Ellipse**	**Cartesian Units**
1	Centre (X, Y)	13.5, 11
2	Major Axis	8
3	Minor Axis	4
4	The inclination of Major Axis with Horizontal in Degrees	-35
S No	**Circle**	**Cartesian Units**
1	Centre (X, Y)	7, 7
2	Radius	6
S No	**Polygon**	**Cartesian Units**
1	V1 (X, Y)	15, 15
2	V2 (X, Y)	17, 13
3	V3 (X, Y)	18, 16
4	V4 (X, Y)	21, 14
5	V5 (X, Y)	18, 20
6	V6 (X, Y)	17, 17
7	V7 (X, Y)	15, 17

5.7.1 Analytical Solution

By using mathematical protocols CCT and CRF, results are calculated. Figures 5.14 to 5.16 shows the graphical results, whereas Table 5.17 the output path. The optimum is 29.84 left-left-left path.

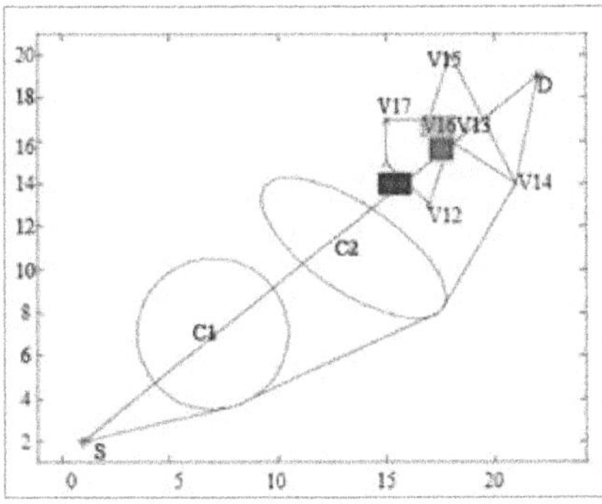

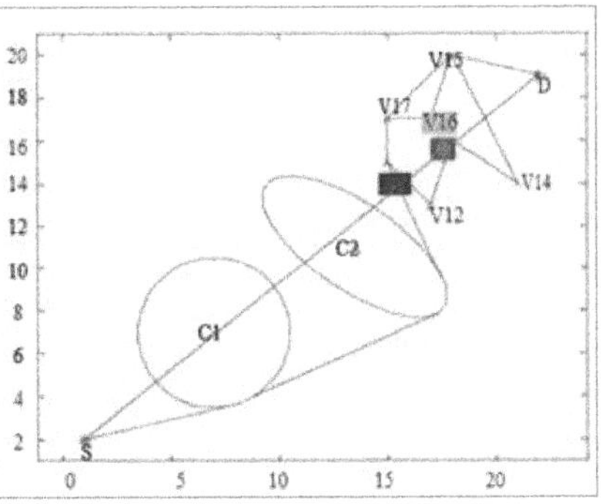

a. Right-Right-Right Path

b. Right-Right-Left Path

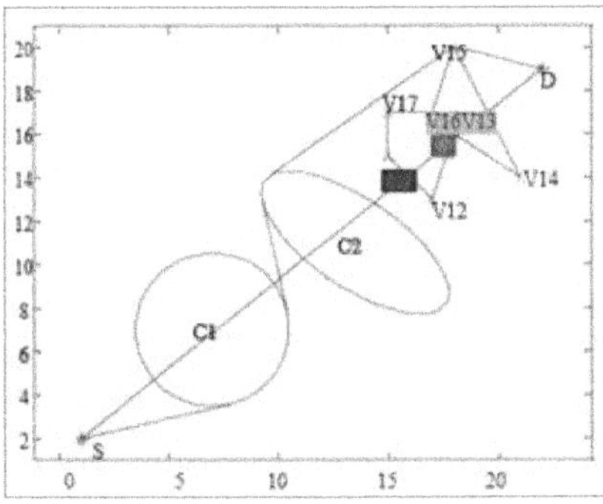

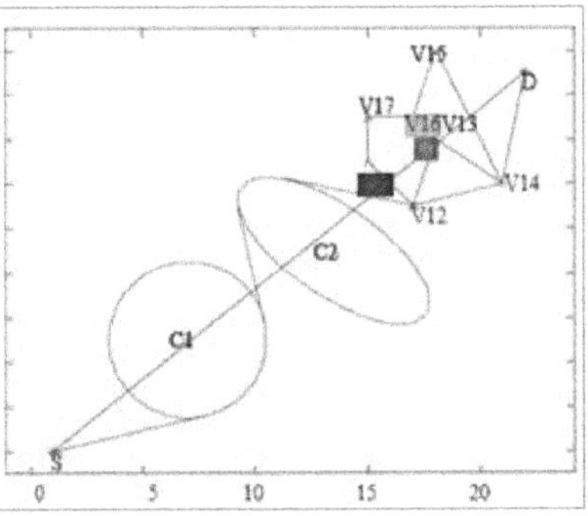

c. Right-Left-Left Path

d. Right-Left-Right Path

Figure 5.14: Graphical Results for Test Case 10 (Part A)

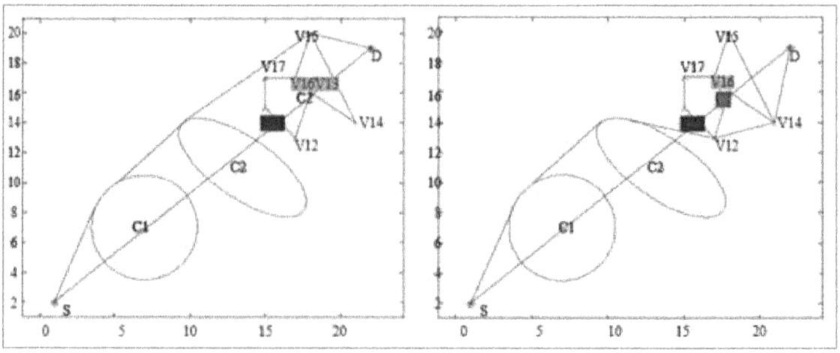

a. Left-Left-Left Path b. Left-Left-Right Path

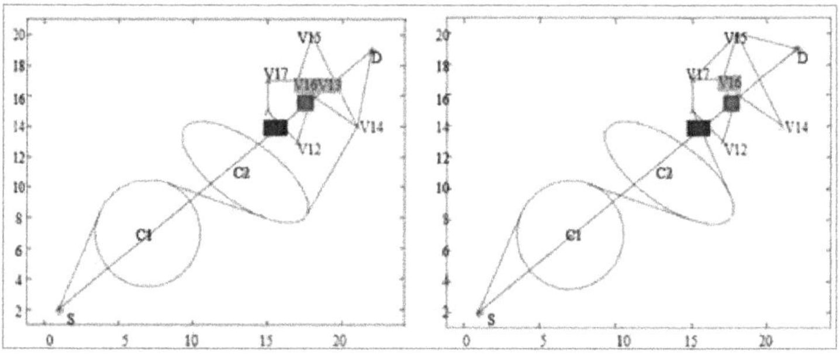

c. Left-Right-Right Path d. Left-Right-Left Path

Figure 5.15: Graphical Results for Test Case 10 (Part B)

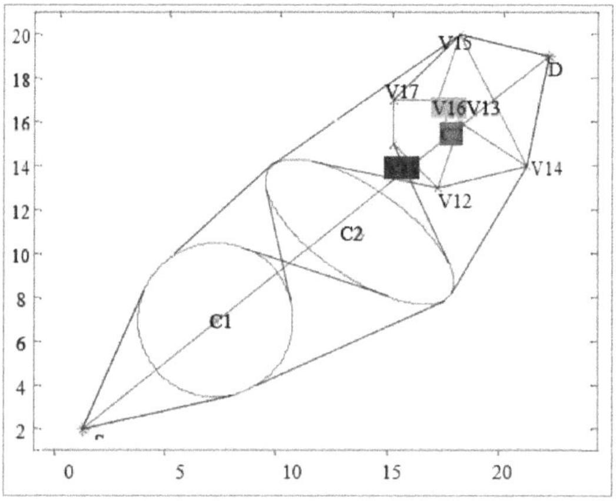

Figure 5.16: Combined Graphical Results for Test Case 10 (All Eight combinations)

Table 5.17: Analytical Results for Test Case 10

Path obtained from 2D3DPP/CCT and CRF Protocol		
Path No.	**Path Direction**	**Length of the Path in Units**
1	Right-Right-Right Path	43.61
2	Right-Right-Left Path	47.21
3	Right-Left-Left Path	33.44
4	Right-Left-Right Path	35.45
5	Left- Left-Left Path	29.84
6	Left-Left-Right Path	32.28
7	Left-Right-Right Path	34.23
8	Left-Right-Left Path	39.09

5.7.2 Experimental Solution

Experimental setup prepared for the point robot avoids collision against the obstacles mentioned in 5.7. The results of the experimentation are tabulated in Table 5.18. A right-right-right path of 36.43 Cartesian units is the best of all three iterations.

Table 5.18: Experimental Results for Test Case 10

Path from the Experiment (Reactive Technique Based)		
Iteration No.	**Path Direction**	**Length of the Path normalized to Cartesian Units**
1	Right-Right-Right Path	36.43
2	Right-Right-Right Path	38.96
3	Right-Right-Right Path	37.20

5.7.3 Simulation Solution

32.34 units right-right-right path is the result obtained through the V-REP® simulator. The graphical path is shown in Figure 5.17.

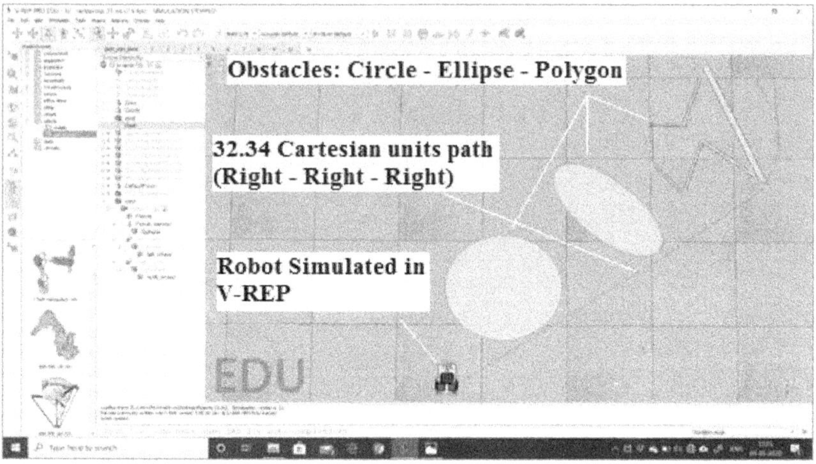

Figure 5.17: Simulation Path for Test Case 10

5.8 Test Case 11: Ellipse-Polygon-Ellipse Obstacle

The input data for the robot and the obstacles is provided in Table 5.19. The obstacles are two ellipses with a polygon in between.

5.8.1 Analytical Solution

The results are found by applying the protocols CRF and CCT and tabulated in Table 5.20. The graphical paths are shown in Figures 5.18 to 5.20. 26.77 right-right-right is the optimum path.

5.8.2 Experimental Solution

The results of the experiment are tabulated in Table 5.21. A right-right-right path of 34.36 Cartesian units is the best of all three iterations.

Table 5.19: Input Data for Test Case 11

S No	Robot	Cartesian Units
1	Source (X, Y)	3, 2
2	Destination (X, Y)	22, 19
S No	**Ellipse 1**	**Cartesian Units**
1	Centre (X, Y)	7, 6
2	Major Axis	6
3	Minor Axis	3
4	The inclination of Major Axis with Horizontal in Degrees	1
S No	**Ellipse 2**	**Cartesian Units**
1	Centre (X, Y)	19, 6
2	Major Axis	6
3	Minor Axis	3
4	The inclination of Major Axis with Horizontal in Degrees	35
S No	**Polygon**	**Cartesian Units**
1	V1 (X, Y)	12, 9
2	V2 (X, Y)	15, 10
3	V3 (X, Y)	15, 13
4	V4 (X, Y)	12, 14
5	V5 (X, Y)	10, 11

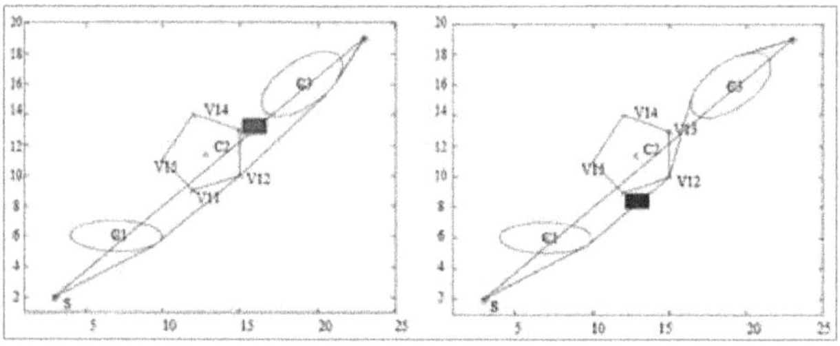

a. Right-Right-Right Path　　　　b. Right-Right-Left Path

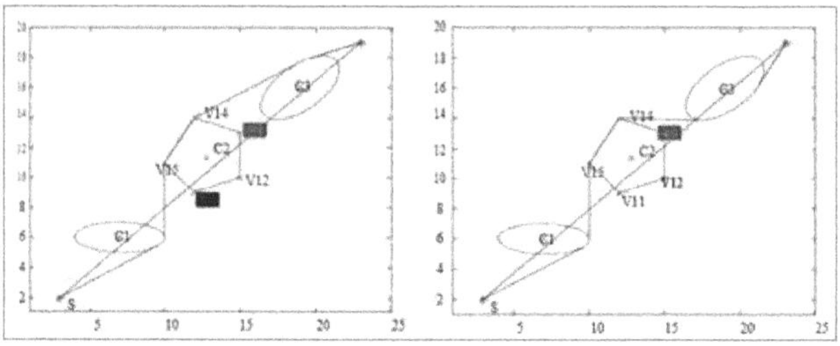

c. Right-Left-Left Path　　　　d. Right-Left-Right Path

Figure 5.18: Graphical Results for Test Case 11 (Part A)

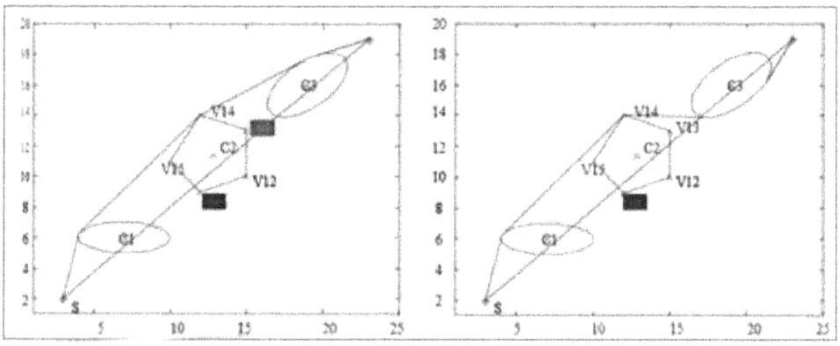

a. Left-Left-Left Path　　　　b. Left-Left-Right Path

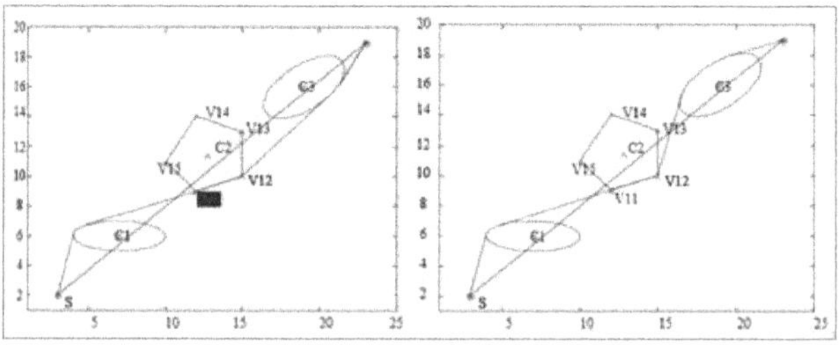

c. Left-Right-Right Path　　　　d. Left-Right-Left Path

Figure 5.19: Graphical Results for Test Case 11 (Part B)

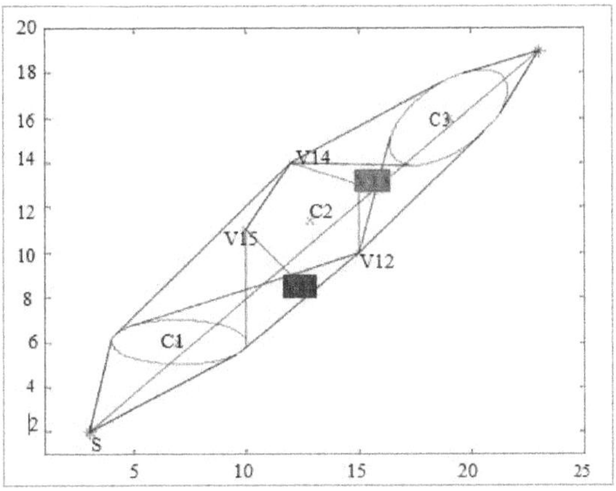

Figure 5.20: Combined Graphical Results for Test Case 11 (All Eight combinations)

Table 5.20: Analytical Results for Test Case 11

Path obtained from 2D3DPP/CCT and CRF Protocol		
Path No.	**Path Direction**	**Length of the Path in Units**
1	Right-Right-Right Path	26.77
2	Right-Right-Left Path	28.13
3	Right-Left-Left Path	30.96
4	Right-Left-Right Path	30.93
5	Left- Left-Left Path	29.66
6	Left-Left-Right Path	29.62
7	Left-Right-Right Path	28.29
8	Left-Right-Left Path	29.66

Table 5.21: Experimental Results for Test Case 11

Path from the Experiment (Reactive Technique Based)		
Iteration No.	**Path Direction**	**Length of the Path normalized to Cartesian Units**
1	Right-Right-Right Path	34.40
2	Right-Right-Right Path	34.64
3	Right-Right-Right Path	34.36

5.8.3 Simulation Solution

28.48 units right-right-right path is the result obtained through the V-REP® simulator. The graphical path is shown in Figure 5.21.

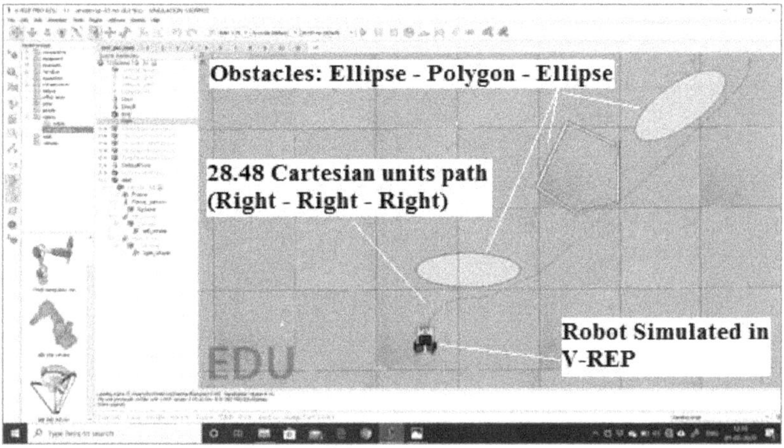

Figure 5.21: Simulation Path for Test Case 11

Table 5.22: Comparative Table for Test Cases 5- 11

Test Case	Test Case Description		Mathematical (Classical) Used and Path obtained		Path obtained from Reactive Technique based Experiment	Path obtained from the V-REP®	% Increase for Experiment over Analytical	% Increase for Simulation over Analytical
	Robot Description	Obstacle Description						
5	A two-dimensional planar environment with a robot moving against	Robot crossing an ellipse and a polygon	2D3DPP / CCT and CRF	17.94	22.46	18.47	25.20	2.95
6		A polygonal and elliptical obstacle in the robot's path	2D3DPP / CCT and CRF	20.29	26.36	23.46	29.92	15.62
7		Obstacles: A polygon and a circle	2D3DPP / CCT and CRF	20.65	27.2	23.58	31.72	14.19
8		Two polygonal and a circular obstacle in the robot's path	2D3DPP / CCT and CRF	24.32	30.42	27.46	25.08	12.91
9		Robot crosses over two polygons and an ellipse	2D3DPP / CCT and CRF	24.9	29.46	27.24	18.31	9.40
10		The obstacles are a circle, an ellipse, and a polygon	2D3DPP / CCT and CRF	29.84	36.43	32.34	22.08	8.38
11		An elliptical - polygonal - elliptical obstacle combination in the robot's path	2D3DPP / CCT and CRF	26.77	34.36	28.48	28.35	6.39

5.9 Summary

CCT protocol, in combination with CRF protocol, is evaluated for robot traversal and obstacle avoidance in a two-dimensional planar arena with static elliptical, circular, and polygonal obstacles. This chapter's findings can be applied to multi-robots. The disadvantage of this chapter is the amount of input data necessary to create the obstacles. The combined algorithm of CCT and CRF is the chapter's research strength.

5.10 Conclusions

This chapter presents seven test cases (Test Case 5 - 11) for identifying collision-free routes for robots in the presence of elliptical, circular, and/or polygonal obstacles. The findings of the analytical, experimental, and simulation approaches show that analytical solutions provide the shortest distance pathways, whereas experimental results provide the longest distance courses. It is also discovered that the increase in path lengths of experimental results over analytical solutions ranges from 18% to 32%, as shown in Table 5.22. The experimental method relies on the detection of infrared obstacles. The percent increase in experimenting is caused by the obstacles combination i.e., polygons and ellipses/circles, their size, shape and orientation. Depending on the configuration space and shape of the barriers, simulation increases path lengths by around 3% to 16% above analytical solutions. The V-Rep® results are on higher side.

Chapter 6

Two-dimensional Path calculation of a Robot against a Dynamic Obstacle

In this chapter, various cases for a robot (robot 1 or the slave robot) moving on a planar path against another identical robot (robot 2 or the master robot) are tested using the mathematical protocol MPD technique. Robot 2 takes its path without deviation, whereobot 1 deviates from its path to avoid the collision. The MPD technique is coded in MATLAB®. Robot 1 is taken as a point robot, and its radius is added to robot 2.

A GSM (global system for mobile communication) protocol is executed to input the two end coordinates sent from a commercial mobile phone to robot 2 (the master robot). Robot 2, retaining its end location, sends on the other end location to robot 2 using the wireless communication system - Zigbee. Both the robots start moving towards their end positions while continue communicating with each other. In the event of a collision, the master robot continues on its path, and the slave avoids collision by diverting from its path. Thus, a cooperative organization of independent robots that interacts with each other and reaches their endpoints without collision is executed. Knowing their own current locations because of the GPS systems embedded on-board and having the end positions, the robots crosscheck their locations and traverse towards the endpoint location. The Zigbee wireless communication system helps them to communicate in real-time. The experimentation is held in the lines of reactive PSO algorithms at the Basketball Court of MVGR College of Engineering (A). Each experiment has been done three times, and the best path is selected.

For experimentation, a scale of 1 Cartesian unit = 250 mm is employed. Because the imaginary circumscribed circle of each robot is 500 mm, accordingly, paths are selected. For simulation, the V-REP® simulator is used. Normalized units are considered for experimentation.

6.1 Test Case Validation

Three test cases are carried out in this chapter (Test Cases 12 - 14). The obstacle in this chapter is an identical robot, which makes the scene a two-dimensional dynamic environment. All test cases with arbitrary input values are evaluated using the classical MPD protocol and the V-REP® simulator. A PSO mimic reactive-based experiment is conducted with the normalized input data. The first test case is when both the robots moving at an angle of 15^0, with a probable collision at their bisection point, the second is when the unconstrained path of one robot is a perpendicular bisector to the other, and the third is when both the robots are moving face-to-face.

6.2 Test Case 12: When the Unconstrained Paths of both the Robots with an internal angle of 15^0 bisect each other

The starting point and endpoint of both the robots are mentioned in Table 6.1. Both the robots move with an angle of 15^0 in between until they reach a point of collision. From this position the robot 1 deviates from avoiding collision, giving straight way to robot 2.

Table 6.1: Input Data for Test Case 12

S No	Robot 1 (The Slave Robot)	Cartesian Units	GPS Coordinates for Experimentation
1	Starting point	(X, Y) 10.51, 6.11	GPS 18.059619, 83.406037
2	Endpoint	(X, Y) 39.48, 13.88	GPS 18.059772, 83.406018
S No	**Robot 2 (The Master Robot)**	**Cartesian Units**	**GPS Coordinates for Experimentation**
1	Starting point	(X, Y) 10, 10	GPS 18.059620, 83.406000
2	Endpoint	(X, Y) 40, 10	GPS 18.059749, 83.406041

6.2.1 Analytical Solution

Results are calculated by using MPD protocol via code written in MATLAB® with graphical presentation. The graphical results from the MATLAB® are shown in Figure 6.1 and analytical results in Table 6.2 for right and left paths. The left path result with 35.29 Cartesian units is the new path for robot 1 (the slave robot).

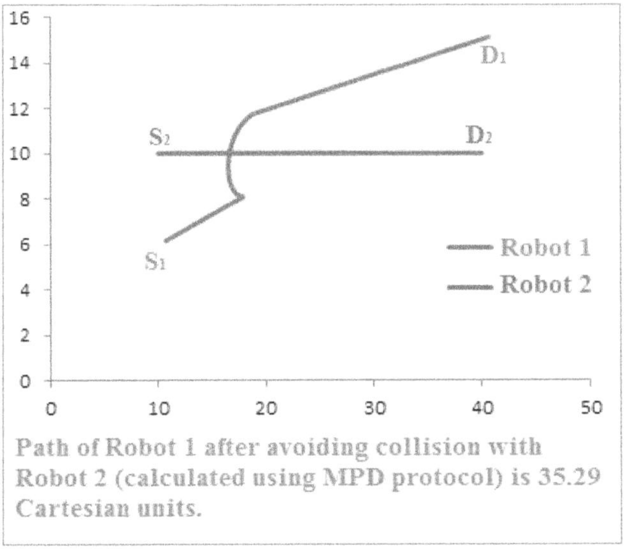

Figure 6.1: Graphical Results for Test Case 12

Table 6.2: Analytical Results for Test Case 12

Path of the Robot 1 (The Slave Robot) obtained from MPD Protocol		
Path No.	**Path Direction**	**Length of the Path in Units**
1	Left Path	35.29

6.2.2 Experimental Solution

As stated in Section 6.1, a 30 unit Cartesian unconstrained route is 7.5 m in length for the experiment. On the arena (Basketball Court), an experimental configuration for both robots with unconstrained routes of 7.5 m is marked. Their likely collision occurs at their un-constrained path's central location. These un-constrained paths are making an included angle of 15^0. The GPS coordinates of these beginning and ending positions (as defined in Table 6.1) are given as input to the robots through GSM, and the results are summarised in Table 6.3. A left path of 42.64 Cartesian units is the best of all three iterations. Figures 6.2 and 6.3 show the experimental snapshots.

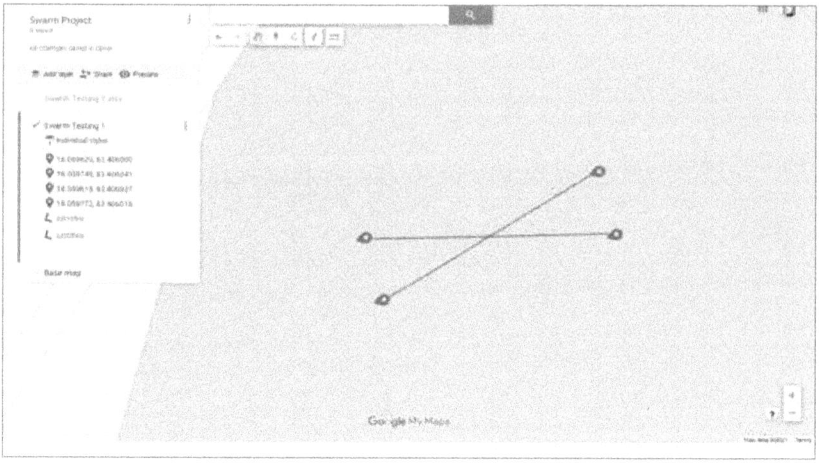

Figure 6.2: Experimental Setup for Test Case 12/GPS Locations as Input (Courtesy: Google Maps ®)

Figure 6.3: Experimental Setup for Test Case 12

Table 6.3: Experimental Results for Test Case 12

Path of the Robot 1 – the Slave Robot from the Experiment (Reactive Technique Based)		
Iteration No.	**Path Direction**	**Length of the Path normalized to Cartesian Units**
1	Left Path	42.64
2	Left Path	46.43
3	Left Path	47.46

6.2.3 Simulation Solution

The path is created using V-REP® for the input data listed in Table 6.1, and the graphic plot is presented in Figure 6.4. The simulation resulted in a path length of 36.30 units (Left Path).

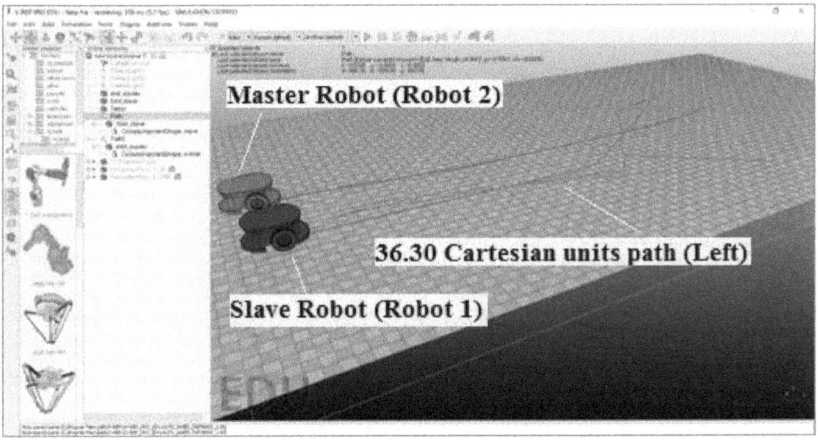

Figure 6.4: V-REP® Simulation path for Test Case 12

6.3 Test Case 13: When the perpendicular Unconstrained Paths of both the Robots bisect each other

The robots move perpendicular to each other, with a possibility of collision exactly at the centre. Robot 1 deviates accordingly, giving way to robot 2. The starting point and endpoint of both the robots are mentioned in Table 6.4.

Table 6.4: Input Data for Test Case 13

S No	Robot 1 (The Slave Robot)	Cartesian Units	GPS Coordinates
1	Starting point	(X, Y) 15, 5	GPS 18.0596352, 83.4060319
2	Endpoint	(X, Y) 15, 15	GPS 18.0596489, 83.4059834
S No	**Robot 2 (The Master Robot)**	**Cartesian Units**	**GPS Coordinates**
1	Starting point	(X, Y) 10, 10	GPS 18.059620, 83.406000
2	Endpoint	(X, Y) 20, 10	GPS 18.059663, 83.406014

6.3.1 Analytical Solution

Results are calculated by using MPD protocol via code written in MATLAB® with graphical presentation. The graphical results from the MATLAB® are shown in Figure 6.5 and analytical results in Table 6.5 for right and left paths. The left path result with 13.30 Cartesian units is the new path for robot 1 (the slave robot).

6.3.2 Experimental Solution

A 10 unit Cartesian unconstrained path is 2.5 m in length for the experiment. The robots are moving perpendicular to each other, with a likely collision at their bisection point. The GPS coordinates of these beginning and ending positions (as defined in Table 6.4) are given as input to the robots through GSM, and the results are summarised in Table 6.6. A left path of 22.41 Cartesian units is the best of all three iterations. The experimental setup is shown in Figures 6.6 and 6.7.

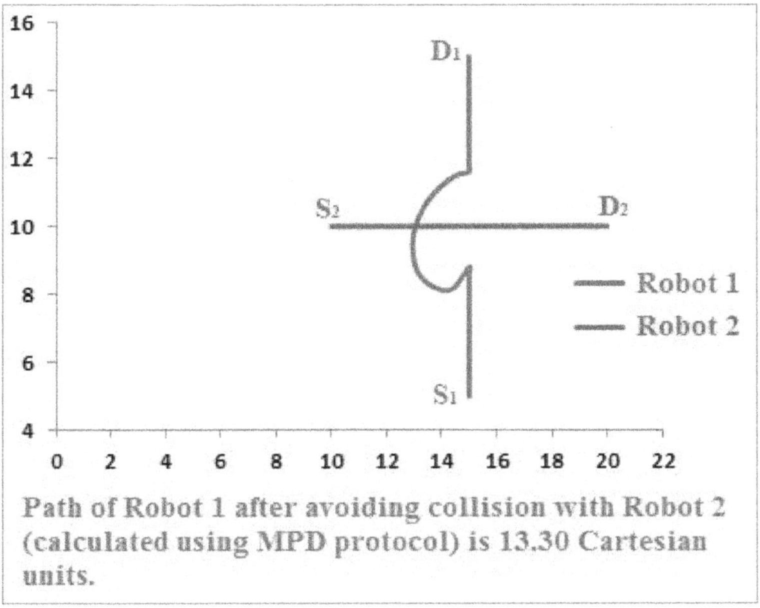

Figure 6.5: Graphical Results for Test Case 13

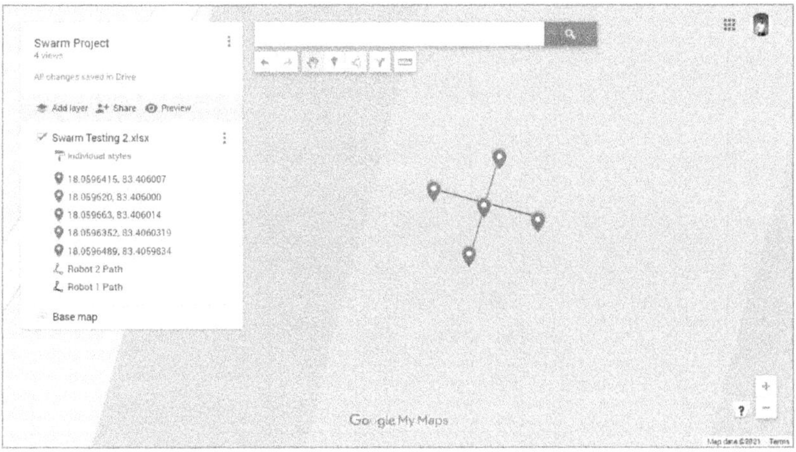

Figure 6.6: Experimental Setup for Test Case 13/GPS Locations as Input (Courtesy: Google Maps ®)

Table 6.5: Analytical Results for Test Case 13

Path of the Robot 1 (The Slave Robot) obtained from MPD Protocol		
Path No.	**Path Direction**	**Length of the Path in Units**
1	Left Path	13.30

Figure 6.7: Experimental Setup for Test Case 13

Table 6.6: Experimental Results for Test Case 13

Path of the Robot 1 – the Slave Robot from the Experiment (Reactive Technique Based)		
Iteration No.	**Path Direction**	**Length of the Path normalized to Cartesian Units**
1	Left Path	23.96
2	Left Path	22.41
3	Left Path	24.38

6.3.3 Simulation Solution

The path is created using V-REP® for the input data listed in Table 6.4, and the graphic plot with source and destination interchanged for Robot 1 is presented in Figure 6.8. The length of the path obtained from the simulation is 16.40 Units (Left Path – The path is mirrored as the source and destination points are switched.)

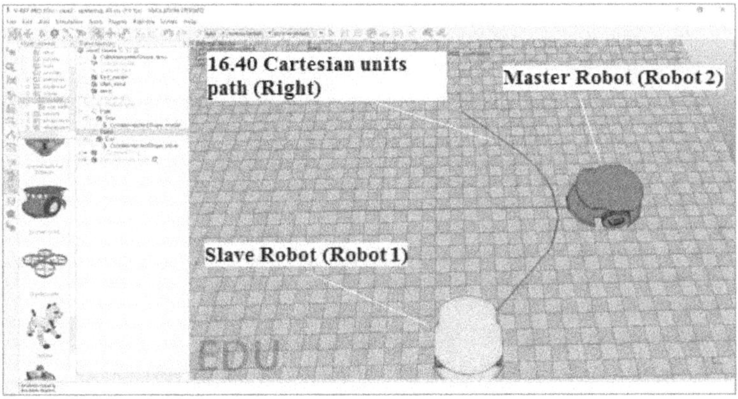

Figure 6.8: V-REP® Simulation path for Test Case 13

6.4 Test Case 14: Both the Robots take on face to face

The robots move face to face, with a possibility of collision exactly at the centre. Robot 1 deviates accordingly, giving way to robot 2. The starting point and endpoint of both the robots are mentioned in Table 6.7.

Table 6.7: Input Data for Test Case 14

S No	Robot 1 (The Slave Robot)	Cartesian Units	GPS Coordinates
1	Starting point	(X, Y) 20, 10	GPS 18.059663, 83.406014
2	Endpoint	(X, Y) 10, 10	GPS 18.059620, 83.406000
S No	**Robot 2 (The Master Robot)**	**Cartesian Units**	**GPS Coordinates**
1	Starting point	(X, Y) 10, 10	GPS 18.059620, 83.406000
2	Endpoint	(X, Y) 20, 10	GPS 18.059663, 83.406014

6.4.1 Analytical Solution

MATLAB® program of the MPD protocol is used to find out the results. The graphical results from the MATLAB® are shown in Figure 6.9 and analytical results in Table 6.8 for right and left paths. The left path result with 13.45 Cartesian units is the new path for robot 1 (the slave robot).

Table 6.8: Analytical Results for Test Case 14

Path of the Robot 1 (The Slave Robot) obtained from MPD Protocol		
Path No.	**Path Direction**	**Length of the Path in Units**
1	Left Path	13.45

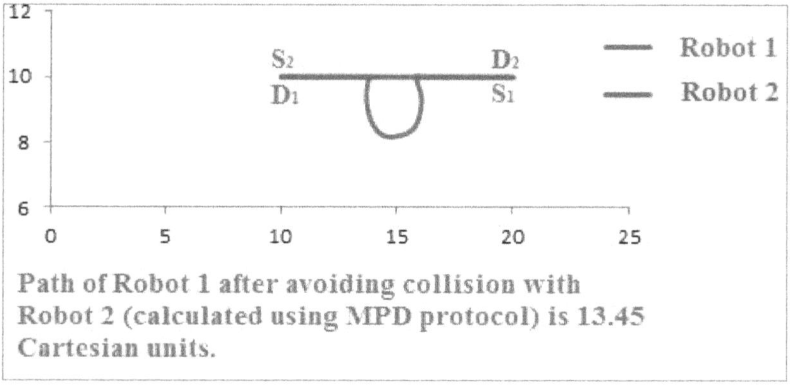

Figure 6.9: Graphical Results for Test Case 14

6.4.2 Experimental Solution

For the experiment, a 10 unit Cartesian unconstrained route is 2.5 m long. The robots are travelling head-on, with a possible collision at their centre point. The GPS coordinates of these starting and stopping points (as described in Table 6.7) are passed onto robots through GSM, and the results are summarised in Table 6.9. A left path of

23.60 Cartesian units is the best of all three iterations. The experimental setup is shown in Figure 6.10.

Figure 6.10: Experimental Setup for Test Case 14/GPS Locations as Input (Courtesy: Google Maps ®)

Table 6.9: Experimental Results for Test Case 14

Path of the Robot 1 – the Slave Robot from the Experiment (Reactive Technique Based)		
Iteration No.	**Path Direction**	**Length of the Path normalized to Cartesian Units**
1	Left Path	23.60
2	Left Path	24.41
3	Left Path	24.38

6.4.3 Simulation Solution

Regarding the input data mentioned in Table 6.7, the path is generated using V-REP®, and the graphic plot is shown in Figure 6.11. The length of the path obtained from the simulation is 15.64 Units (Left Path).

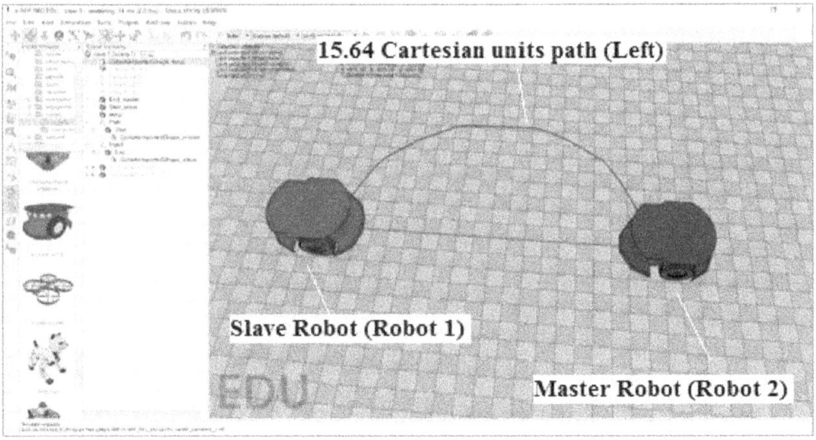

Figure 6.11: V-REP® Simulation path for Test Case 14

6.5 Summary

Dynamic route planning for two mobile robots is demonstrated using the MPD MATLAB® code. PSO was investigated and used in experiments. Paths were simulated using the V-REP® simulator. This research can be expanded to include more than two robots. The disadvantage of this research is that it does not allow for testing the performance of the robots when static obstacles are also included in the path. The MPD technique is the study's distinguishing characteristic. MPD is effective for driverless cars, defence robots. The use of the MPD protocol for UAVs and AUVs is a strong suggestion based on the chapter's study.

6.6 Conclusions

This chapter includes three test cases (Test Case 12 - 14) for identifying collision-free robot pathways in the presence of another identical robot as a dynamic obstacle. Analytical, experimental, and simulation studies reveal that analytical solutions provide the shortest distance courses, but experimental results yield the longest distance paths. Furthermore, it is observed that the increase in path lengths of experimental results over analytical solutions ranges from 20% to 76%. The % increase was also impacted by the robots' size, their directions, as illustrated in the instance of a head-to-head collision.

Depending on the configuration space and geometry of the obstacles, simulation increases path lengths by 2% to 24% over analytical solutions.

Table 6.10: Comparative Table for Test Cases 12- 14

Test Case	Test Case Description		Mathematical (Classical) Protocol Used and Path obtained		Path obtained from Reactive Technique based Experiment	Path obtained from the V-REP®	% Increase for Experiment over Analytical	% Increase for Simulation over Analytical
	Robot Description	Obstacle Description						
12	The slave robot moving in a two-dimensional planar environment	Crossing with the master robot in a 2D planar arena with an angle of 15 degrees with slave robot path	MPD	35.29	42.64	36.3	20.83	2.86
13		The master robot is moving at an angle of 90 degrees	MPD	13.3	22.41	16.4	68.50	23.31
14		Head to head collision with the master robot	MPD	13.45	23.6	15.64	75.46	16.28

Chapter 7

Three-dimensional Path calculation of an Autonomous Underwater Vehicle against a Static Obstacle

Survey, substantiation and plotting of three-dimensional underwater conditions are the biggest challenges in path planning. As per a 2018 report of the National Oceanic and Atmospheric Administration (NOAA), 80% of the underwater environment is unexplored. An underwater environment can be a natural underwater cave, a plant, a submerged manmade object that makes the exploration fascinating, complex and dangerous.

The band limit available for underwater communication is minimal and re-echoing, leading to issues of reliability. High-frequency communication in shallow water is a highly challenging task because underwater medium distorts signal properties.

Three-dimensional environment path planning exhibits a great scope, but unlike two-dimensional environment, the complexity gets bigger exponentially with springy constraints. Even though path planning is time-consuming and tedious in such complex three-dimensional environments but once achieved will lay a path for a fascinating underwater exploration.

Underwater maintenance, monitoring, and reconnaissance are impossible due to the ocean's deepest recesses and the hospitability of this environment for humanity. The advent of different underwater vehicles during the last half-century has aided in the resolution of these difficulties. Unmanned Untethered Vehicles (UUVs), Remotely Operated Vehicles (ROVs), and Autonomous Profiling Vehicles (AVPs) are examples of these vehicles.

Radio-controlled vehicles (RCVs) utilise a cable to link an underwater vehicle to a sea-level vehicle. The tether supplies the vehicle with power and control signals as well as relaying data to the operator. Unmanned Untethered Vehicles (UUVs) have eliminated the tether's vulnerabilities. The tether is substituted with an optical, acoustic or electromagnetic link to the sea level vehicle in these UUVs. The UUVs' utility was significantly constrained due to the slow data transmission speeds available for submersible vessels and their narrow communications range. Autonomous vehicles, which replace the need for external operator control with vehicle-based controls, solve the limitations of UUVs. Autonomous Profiling Vehicles (APVs) were able to function without human assistance; however, their movement was restricted to basic vertical motions in a water column.

AUVs are self-propelled underwater vehicles that function autonomously utilising control signals provided by an onboard computer system. Without the requirement for operator control, AUVs satisfy the demand for mobility in all three dimensions inside an ocean environment. The hull, navigation, control, communications, and sensor subsystem enhancements have all been the subject of recent technological advances. Reprogramming the AUV and retrieving gathered information both need communication with the AUV. First, the vehicle's movement is constrained by the float and attachment cable, which increases the possibility of cable snags while operating in restricted waters, and second, the float does not always extend far enough above the surface of the water, resulting in a lower range and transmission quality. AUVs are frequently equipped with a range of sensors that enable them to detect their location and collect measurements in the water.

Considering the current day systems, it has been observed that there are many drawbacks and shortcomings leading to failed missions and unreliable or insufficient data. The lack of multipurpose systems leads to tedious and expensive exploration, maintenance and reconnaissance activities. Legacy communication systems often tend to fail, leading to ambiguity and reliability issues, thereby contributing to extended timelines and unreliable data. A significant percentage of the current day systems do not facilitate higher fuel capacities or battery power backups to support prolonged underwater activities without the need to resurface often. The fully automated systems being used today have proven to have shortcomings that require human intervention constantly, which is a complex process during an ongoing mission or activity.

7.1 Test Case Validation

In this chapter, a case of an underwater robot moving on a spatial path against a submerged cylindrical obstacle is tested using the mathematical protocols 2D3DPP,

SLICE, CCT and CRF. The robot deviates from its path to avoid collision with the cylindrical obstacle. The protocols are coded in MATLAB®. For analytical calculation, the robot is taken as a point robot, and its radius is added to the cylinder.

A tethered controlled underwater robot is fabricated for the experiment. A program is written in Arduino language with the toolbox to move the robot one step forward and one step down. Four electrical DC motors of 12 V and 18000 RPM (two for y-axis up and down movement and two for XZ plane forward and backward movement), an IRF MOSFET H-Bridge motor driver, a 12 V lithium-ion polymer battery are used. A PVC pipe of 63 mm diameter and 300 mm length is selected for the robot keeping in mind all the components it has to accommodate. The robot has a waterproof ultrasonic sensor to detect obstacles. Normalized units are considered for experimentation. Experimentation is conducted in the pool of MVGR College of Engineering.

7.2 Test Case 15: An AUV with a Static Cylindrical Obstacle

The starting point and endpoint of the robot, the position and dimensions of the cylinder are mentioned in Table 7.1.

Table 7.1: Input Data for Test Case 15

S No	Robot	Cartesian Units
1	Starting point (X, Y, Z)	2, 7, 15
2	Endpoint (X, Y, Z)	32, 7, 5
S No	**Cylinder**	**Cartesian Units**
1	Centre (X, Y, Z)	17, 7, 0
2	Base Circle Diameter	10
3	Height	20

7.2.1 Analytical Solution

Below results are calculated by using 2D3DPP/SLICE/CCT protocol via code written in MATLAB® with graphical presentation. The graphical results from the MATLAB® are shown in Figure 7.1 and analytical results in Table 7.2 for right and left paths. The right-down path result with 41.68 Cartesian units is the unconstrained path for the robot. Figures 7.2 and 7.3 show the illustration for the unconstrained and constrained paths drawn in AutoCAD®.

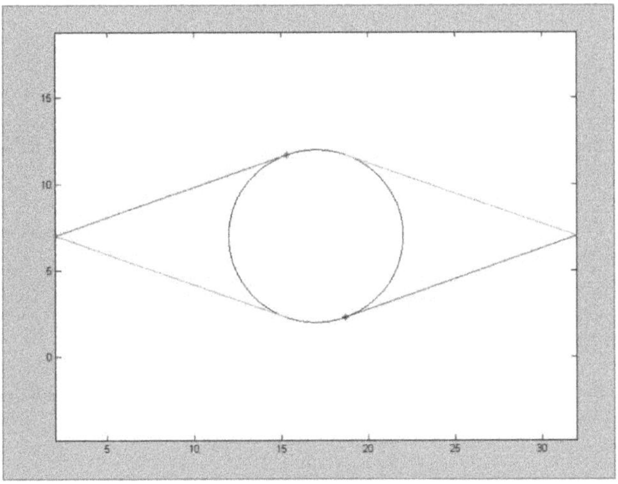

Figure 7.1: Graphical Results for Test Case 15

Table 7.2: Analytical Results for Test Case 15

Path of the Robot obtained from 2D3DPP Protocol			
Path No.	**Path Direction**	**Length of the Planar Path in Units**	**Total Length of the Path after adding Depth Traverse**
1	Left Path	31.68	41.68
2	Right Path	31.68	41.68

7.2.2 Experimental Solution

The robot is assumed to be inscribed inside a circle of 300 mm diameter. As mentioned in Section 7.1, the experimentation is conducted in MVGR College of Engineering's water pool (Water pool dimensions 10 x 10 x 1.2 m). A scale of 1 Cartesian unit equals 60 mm is considered for experimentation. A right path of 44.64 Cartesian units is the best of all three iterations, and results are recorded in Table 7.3. Figures 7.4 to 7.6 show the experimental snapshots.

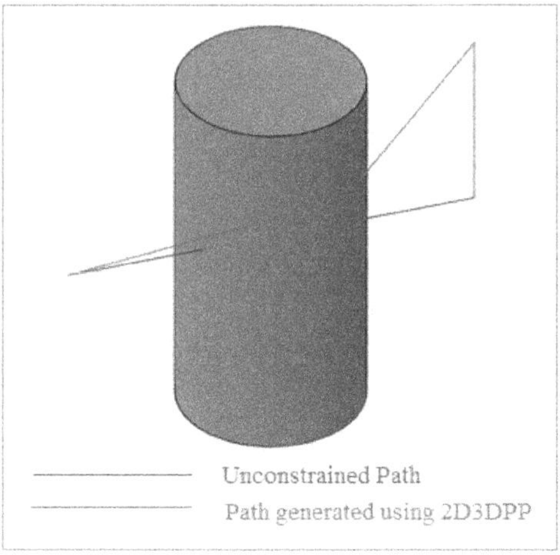

Figure 7.2: Illustration for the unconstrained and constrained paths drawn in AutoCAD®

- Isometric View

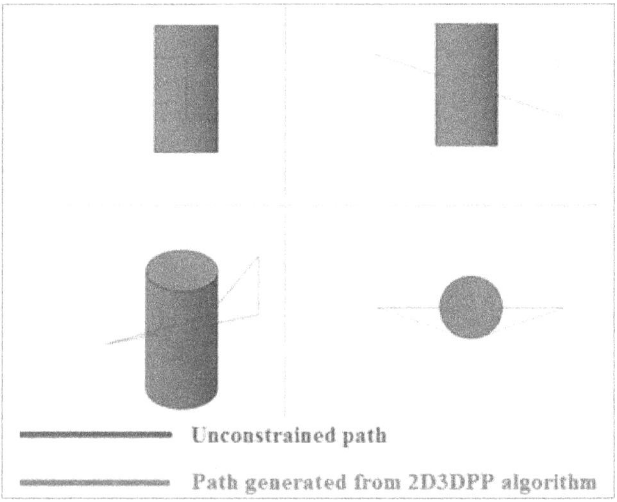

Figure 7.3: Illustration for the unconstrained and constrained paths drawn in AutoCAD®

- All Views

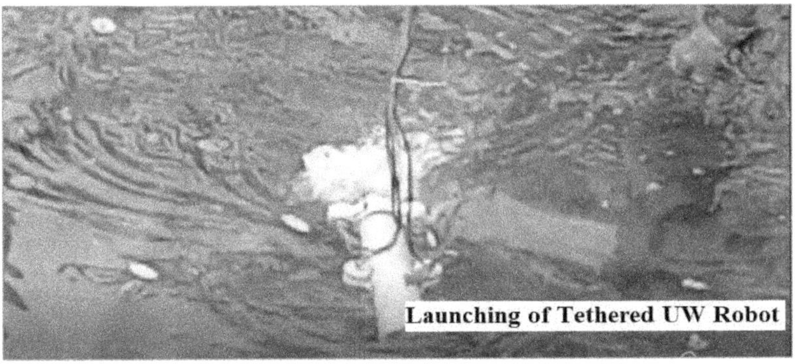

Figure 7.4: AUV launching - On the waterbed

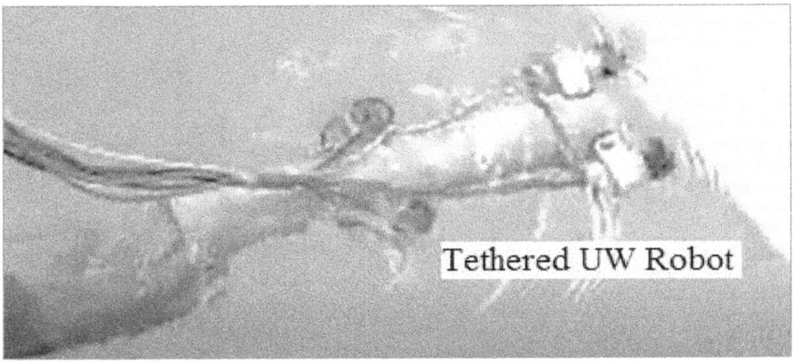

Figure 7.5: AUV moving underwater

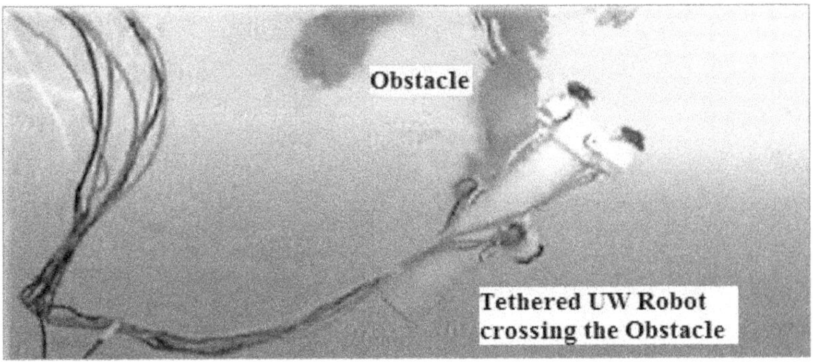

Figure 7.6: AUV crossing the obstacle.

Table 7.3: Experimental Results for Test Case 15

Path of the Robot from the Experiment (Reactive Technique Based)		
Iteration No.	**Path Direction**	**Length of the Path normalized to Cartesian Units**
1	Right Path	44.64
2	Left Path	48.24
3	Left Path	47.04

7.2.3 Simulation Solution

For the input data mentioned in Table 7.1, the path is generated using V-REP®, and the graphic plot is shown in Figure 7.7. The length of the path obtained from the simulation is 38.60 Units (Right - Down Path). Figures 7.2 and 7.3 show the AutoCAD® illustration, and Figure 7.7 to 7.10 show V-REP® results.

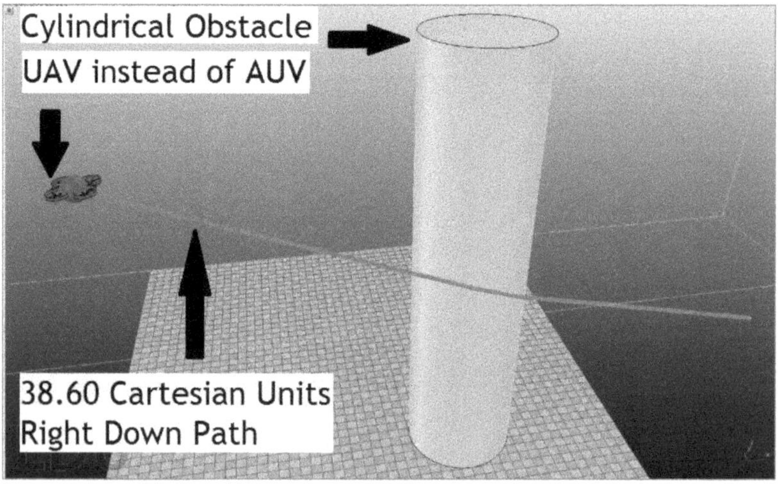

Figure 7.7: V-REP® Simulation for Test Case 15 (Isometric View)

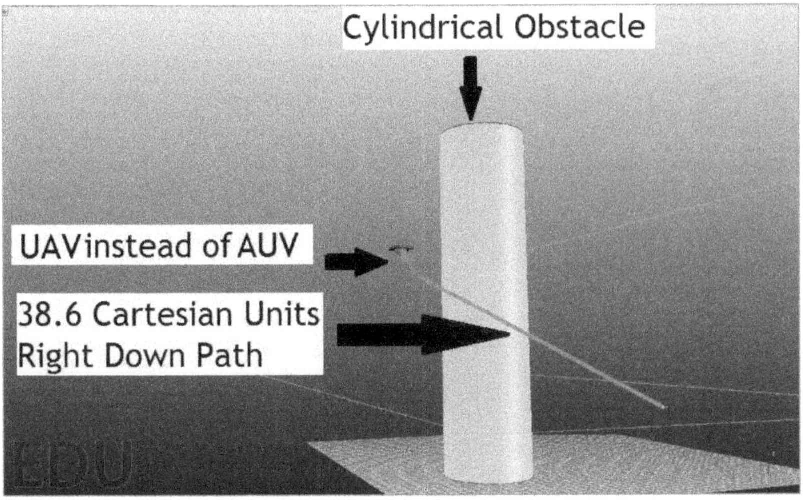

Figure 7.8: V-REP® Simulation for Test Case 15 (Side View)

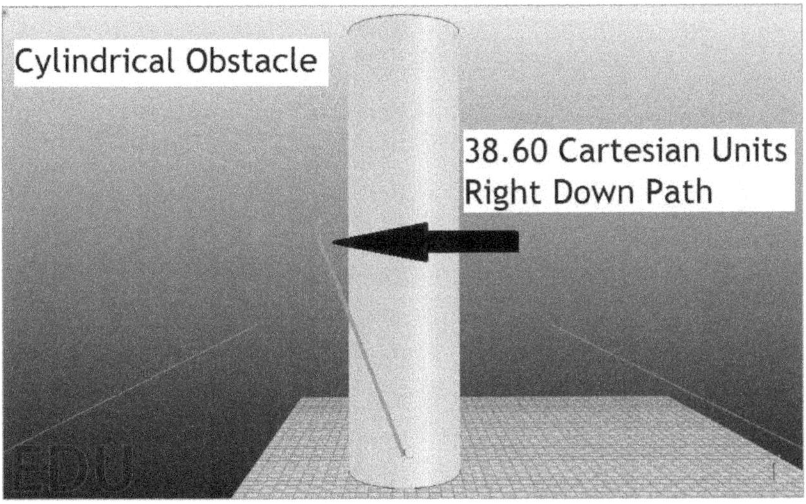

Figure 7.9: V-REP® Simulation for Test Case 15 (Front View)

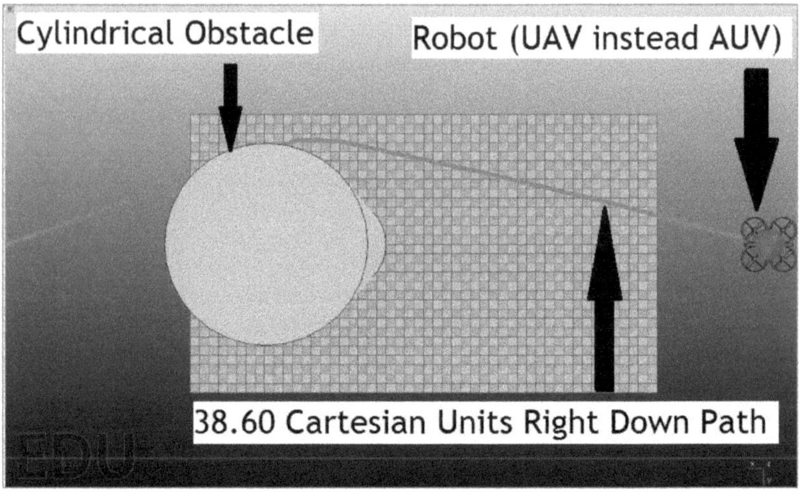

Figure 7.10: V-REP® Simulation for Test Case 15 (Top View)

7.3 Modular Autonomous Underwater Vehicle (MAUV) – A Proposal for International Patent

The present invention relates to autonomous underwater vehicles. In particular, the invention under disclosure relates to semi-autonomous underwater platforms that comprise various modules that are capable of communicating among themselves while performing complex tasks individually or in conjunction.

A modular autonomous underwater vehicle is characterized by a combination of the following modules; a motorized flotation device with payload and communication capabilities, a tethered underwater carrier capable of single-axis displacement and a detachable semi-autonomous module comprising of various sensors that work in conjunction as an autonomous unit performing a given task or as a part of a group of many such entities. The MAUV under disclosure is further characterized by a hybrid navigation protocol 2D3DPP comprising of multistage two dimensional and three-dimensional path planning, an indigenous full-duplex communication protocol that allows for offloaded computation of complex algorithms, tele-control of the entire system, long-range radio frequency communication for localization and rescue purposes, tethered serial communication for transmission of media and short-range ultrasound communication when the detachable module is performing a task autonomously.

The motorised flotation device will be equipped with a single axis pulley system that can lower a payload (detachable semi-autonomous module) underwater in the negative Y direction, as shown in the different views of the docking diagram in Figures 7.13 to 7.15. This may be achieved by a multitude of methods, such as a buoyant engine or motorised pulley system or a hybrid method that will enable the upward and downward movement of the payload in a controlled and precise manner. The underwater carrier is a device equipped with a dispatch mechanism that helps in the process of detachment and attachment of the semi-autonomous unit.

Furthermore, this underwater carrier is characterized by a power management system that is capable of drawing power from the non-submergible sea level carrier, storing the power in a network of batteries/cells and also charging the detachable semi-autonomous unit. In yet another embodiment of the underwater carrier, a pair of propellers arranged in a specific manner act as a counter to the ocean current that may exist at the site of deployment. Furthermore, the underwater carrier also constitutes necessary hardware such as optical encoders, acoustic triangulation sensors and radio waves based scanners that may assist during any particular mission. Figures 7.11 to 7.12 shows the overall block diagram, communication block diagram and the docking system for the proposed model.

7.4 Summary

This chapter examines the concepts of AUVs and how they function. SLICE and the 2D3DPP protocol were created to conduct three-dimensional underwater robot route planning. This research can be expanded to modular AUVs, as mentioned in the patent proposal. The disadvantage of this research is that it cannot evaluate the performance of a robot in natural underwater systems. The research's strength is its steadfast reliance on the 2.5D (SLICE) method. 2D3DPP and SLICE are appropriate for AUVs in the marine industry. The chapter strongly recommends the development of simulators to evaluate the trajectories of AUVs.

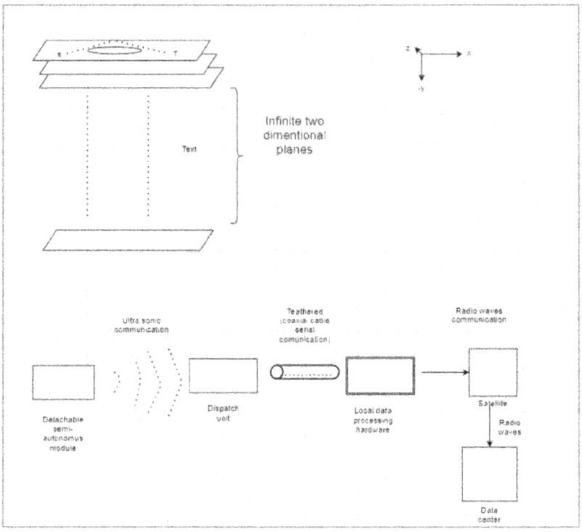

Figure 7.11: A Modular Underwater Vehicle System for Maintenance, Surveillance, and Reconnaissance Operations (Proposal)

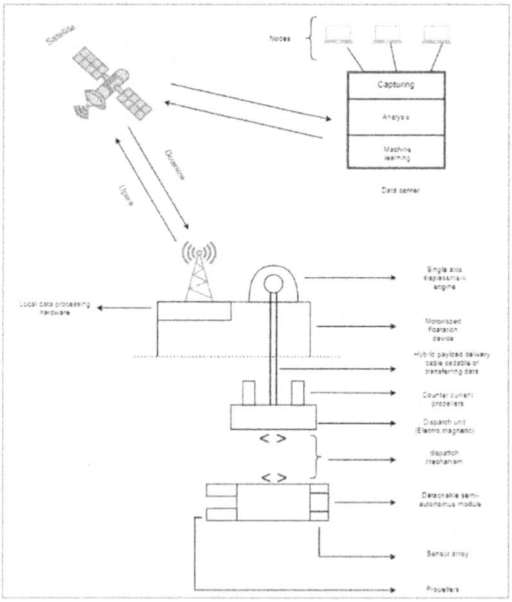

Figure 7.12: Communication Block Diagram

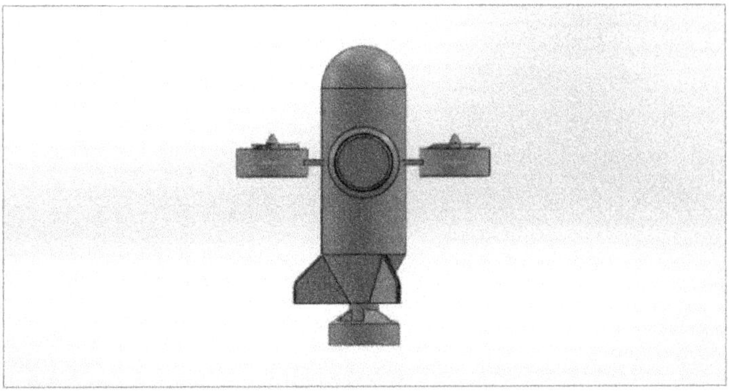

Figure 7.13: Docking System (Top View)

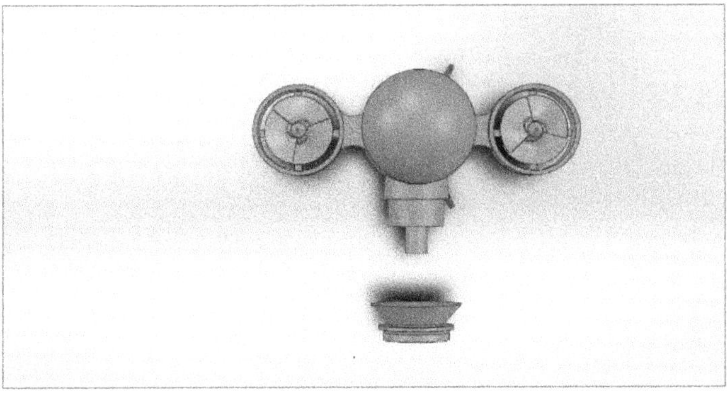

Figure 7.14: Docking System (Front View)

Figure 7.15: Docking System (Isometric View)

7.5 Conclusion

This chapter includes one test case (Test Case 15) for determining a collision-free path for an underwater robot in the presence of a static cylindrical object. The analytical, experimental, and simulation approaches' findings show that simulation solutions provide the shortest distance pathway, whereas experimental results provide the longest distance path. It is also revealed that the experiment result over-analytical solution has a 7% increase in path length. The obstacle detection approach used in the experiment is based on ultrasonic sensors. To compute the shortest distance in the analytical findings, the techniques mentioned above employ 2.5D computational geometry. The percent increase in experimenting is caused by the sensor's reaction time, the actuator motor's response time, the form, size, and orientation of the cylindrical obstacle. Depending on the configuration space and geometry of the barrier, simulation reduces path lengths by approximately 7% compared to the analytical approach.

Table 7.4: Comparative Table for Test Case 15

Test Case	Test Case Description		Mathematical (Classical) Protocol Used and Path obtained		Path obtained from Reactive Technique based Experiment	Path obtained from the V-REP®	% Increase for Experiment over Analytical	% Increase for Simulation over Analytical
	Robot Description	Obstacle Description						
15	A robot moving underwater	A cylindrical obstacle in its path	2D3DPP / SLICE	41.68	44.64	38.6	7.10	-7.39

Chapter 8

Result Analysis

8.1 Result Analysis

Fifteen different test cases are conducted in the four categories, namely path planning of a robot: 1) in a planar environment for a two-dimensional path against static elliptical obstacles, 2) against a combination of elliptical, circular and polygonal obstacles for a two-dimensional planar path 3) in a planar arena avoiding a two-dimensional dynamic obstacle and 4) in underwater spatial arena avoiding a static cylindrical obstacle for a three-dimensional path. Results for all the test cases from classical mathematical protocols, reactive based experimentation and simulation are presented in Table 8.1.

Table 8.1: Comparative Table for all Fifteen Test Cases

Test Case Number	Test Case Description		Mathematical (Classical) Protocol Used and Path obtained	% Increase for Experiment over Analytical	% Increase for Simulation over Analytical
	Robot Description	Obstacle Description			
1	A robot moving in a two-dimensional planar arena	The obstacle is a single ellipse	2D3DPP / CCT	20.92	2.94
2		Two elliptical obstacles in the robot's path	2D3DPP / CCT	31.18	3.93
3			2D3DPP / CCT	25.00	5.54
4		Robot encounters three ellipses	2D3DPP / CCT	19.66	11.84
5		Robot crossing an ellipse and a polygon	2D3DPP / CCT and CRF	25.20	2.95
6	A two-dimensional planar environment with a robot moving against	A polygonal and elliptical obstacle in the robot's path	2D3DPP / CCT and CRF	29.92	15.62
7		Obstacles: A polygon and a circle	2D3DPP / CCT and CRF	31.72	14.19

8		Two polygonal and a circular obstacle in the robot's path	2D3DPP / CCT and CRF	25.08	12.91
9		Robot crosses over two polygons and an ellipse	2D3DPP / CCT and CRF	18.31	9.40
10	Planar Robot	The obstacles are a circle, an ellipse, and a polygon	2D3DPP / CCT and CRF	22.08	8.38
11		An elliptical - polygonal - elliptical obstacle combination in the robot's path	2D3DPP / CCT and CRF	28.35	6.39
12	The slave robot moving in a two-dimensional planar environment	Crossing with the master robot in a 2D planar arena with an included angle of 15 degrees	MPD	20.83	2.86
13		The master robot is moving at an angle of 90 degrees	MPD	68.50	23.31
14		Head to head collision with the master robot	MPD	75.46	16.28
15	A robot moving underwater	A cylindrical obstacle in its path	2D3DPP / SLICE	7.10	-7.39

In chapter 4, four test cases are described for identifying two-dimensional collision-free pathways for robots in the presence of one/two/three ellipses as obstacles. The results show that analytical solutions provide the shortest distance paths, whereas experimental results provide the longest distance paths. It is also observed that the increase in path distances of experimental results over analytical solutions ranges from

18% to 32%. Depending on the configuration space and shape of the obstacles, simulation increases path distances by about 2% to 12% over analytical solutions.

In Chapter 5, seven test cases are presented for determining two-dimensional collision-free robot pathways in the face of elliptical, circular, and polygonal obstacles. Analytical, experimental, and simulation studies reveal that analytical solutions provide the shortest distance paths, and experimental results yield the longest distance paths. Furthermore, it is revealed that the increase in path lengths of experimental results above analytical solutions ranges from 18% to 32%. Simulation increases path lengths by roughly 2% to 16% over analytical solutions, depending on the configuration space and geometry of the barriers.

The sixth chapter contains three test cases for identifying two-dimensional collision-free robot paths in the presence of another identical robot as a dynamic obstacle. Analytical, experimental, and simulation research show that analytical solutions produce the shortest distance paths, whereas experimental results produce the longest distance paths. Furthermore, it has been discovered that the increase in path lengths of experimental results over analytical solutions ranges from 20% to 76%. Simulation increases path lengths by 2% to 24% over analytical methods, depending on the configuration space and geometry of the barriers.

In Chapter 7, one test case is provided for identifying a three-dimensional collision-free path for an underwater robot in the presence of a static cylindrical object. The results of the analytical, experimental, and simulation approaches reveal that simulation solutions provide the shortest distance path, whereas experimental results provide the longest distance path. It is also revealed that the over-analytical solution has a 7% increase in path length for the experiment results. Simulation, depending on the configuration space and shape of the barrier, reduces path lengths by about 7% when compared to the analytical technique.

In 14 of the 15 test situations presented, path lengths obtained by experimentation and simulation are greater than those determined using the analytical (classical) approach. The following factors contribute to the non-uniformity in the % rise of experimental and simulation findings over analytical:

1) The 15 tabulated findings are made up of four different categories. The first category is for a single robot confronting static elliptical obstacles in a planar arena. The second is against ellipses, circles and polygons, which are static mixed barriers. The third category is for two identical mobile robots crossing each other in a planar arena, and the fourth is for an autonomous underwater vehicle moving in a three-dimensional arena versus a stationary cylindrical object.

2) The techniques utilised for analytical findings differ in each of the four groups described above. The CCT technique is utilised to determine the results for the first category, while CCT in conjunction with CRF is used for the second category. In category three, a novel MPD protocol is utilised to test the findings, and in category four, a unified 2D3DPP protocol is employed.

3) Despite the fact that all four groups were subjected to reactive technique-based experimentation, the arrangement was fundamentally different. An IR sensor-based robot is fabricated and tested against obstacles for the first and second categories. In the third category, an experiment based on swarm intelligence is carried out, which has a higher sensitivity than the IR approach. The cylindrical robot is equipped with an ultrasonic sensor for the fourth AUV category. For each experiment, the sizes, shapes, and embedded circuitry are varied and unique.

The aforementioned factors combine to affect the consistency of experimental results in terms of percent increase above analytical results.

4) The V-Rep® simulator is used to replicate all fifteen test situations (four categories). The proprietary methods employed in the V-Rep® simulator are primarily responsible for the non-uniformity in % rise of simulation results over analytical for the first fourteen test cases. V-Rep® does not have an underwater interface in the fourth category (fifteenth test case). As a result, the simulation is carried out in space above the Earth. This is why the simulation result is lower than the analytical result in the test case number 15.

8.2 Summary

Concepts of robotic path planning, its importance for mobile robots are learned in this current research. Different approaches to formulate path planning techniques, their pros and cons, limitations are studied. New mathematical technique CCT is developed for robot traversing, avoiding obstacles in a two-dimensional planar arena crossing static elliptical and or circular obstacles. In combination with CRF, CCT protocol finds the path for mixed elliptical-polygonal obstacles. Using the MPD MATLAB® code, dynamic path planning for two mobile robots is presented, studied about AUVs and their working. Developed SLICE and 2D3DPP protocol to execute three-dimensional underwater robot path planning. Explored PSO and implemented it in experimentation. Simulated paths using V-REP® application software.

This study can be extended to multi-robot operations in multiplex environments, harmonized and networked collaborative robots with different speeds, designing robots with less payload, hybridization between classical and reactive techniques, other simulators, and their working. The limitation of this research is that it cannot evaluate the performance of a robot in natural underwater systems such as rivers, seas, or oceans to determine the precise bottleneck.

The research's strength is its steadfast adherence to traditional methodologies and comparable outcomes. CCT and CRF protocols are beneficial for making robots that can be used for cleaning places like empty classrooms, malls, theatres, grounds, industrial workshops, unmanned warehouses, where most of the obstacles are static. MPD works well in home automation robots, hospitality robots, driverless cars, etc. 2D3DPP and SLICE are suitable for AUVs in underwater maintenance, surveillance, and reconnaissance operations in marine industries.

A strong recommendation from the research is the necessity of hybridization. More benefits in terms of time, money, risk can be achieved from robots that work on mixed path planning techniques.

Chapter 9

Conclusions

9.1 Conclusions

1. Two-dimensional paths obtained from the new mathematical protocols, Curvature Common Tangent (CCT) and in combination with Coordinate Reference Frame (CRF), gave better results for the considered test cases. The advantage of classical techniques, unlike reactive techniques, is in the size and shape of the robot. In reactive techniques, more electronic components are required to control the robot, which increases the robot's weight and subsequently affects its control. On average, results from the mathematical protocol for a robot in a two-dimensional arena with static obstacles are 20% more effective than reactive-based experimental results and 8% than simulation results. These protocols work better in global navigation scenarios.
2. For a robot traversing collision-free from another identical robot, the mathematical technique gives the best path comparing to reactive techniques. On average, a 28% and 12% betterment is found in mathematical results in comparison with reactive technique based experimental and simulation results for dynamic robots path planning. Nevertheless, in practice, reactive techniques are more accessible to implement than classical techniques because of their easy implementation in a complex dynamic system. Even in such a case, a hybrid methodology combining the benefits of both classical techniques and reactive techniques is more appropriate than a standalone reactive or bio-inspired technique.
3. In the case of three-dimensional path planning, complexity increases exponentially with reactive techniques. Even though the optimum result is for the simulation, still the result can be considered in favour of the mathematical approach, as the simulator is not equipped with underwater simulation. The mathematical result is 7% more efficient than the reactive based experimental result for a three-dimensional underwater robot crossing a cylindrical obstacle. A 2.5D approach is an apt method to solve three-dimensional path planning with static obstacles.

4. Even though the V-REP® application software provided good simulation results, but as the software is not open-source software, the algorithms running behind are unknown. Moreover, V-REP® is not equipped with underwater simulation, which is a significant drawback. Lacking good path planning simulators emphasizes an immediate need for open-source application software for robot path planning in any terrain.

9.2 Future Scope

Following are the few aspects of path planning for the researchers to investigate in the future.

1. The present study on a single robot and multi obstacles can be extended to a multi-obstacle, multi-robot operations in complex environments.
2. In dynamic path planning, the current disclosure is about two identical robots with the same speed crossing each other is discussed, which can be further extended for coordinated and networked multi-robotics systems with different speeds.
3. As seen in the experimentation, even though reactive approaches are extra innovative and intellectual for both known and unknown environments, incomplete spatial information continually alters its environment and requires more electronic parts, making the robots bulkier. In the future new embedded components for the design and fabrication of the robot can make it lesser in weight. This subsequently increases the performance.
4. The performance of classic approaches can be enhanced by hybridization with reactive approaches. Future developments can bring customization in robot path planning. In a dynamic environment, there is a scope for new research of a robot for a moving goal problem compared with a moving obstacle problem.
5. For undersea exploration, sea prediction and simulation models, such as MSEAS can be used in future techniques in order to produce reasonable predictions of optimal paths.
6. There is an immediate demand for developing path planning simulators, especially for AUVs.

www.ingramcontent.com/pod-product-compliance
Lightning Source LLC
LaVergne TN
LVHW051922051126
851857LV00021B/2101

* 9 7 9 8 2 5 6 2 6 8 5 8 9 *